7 Steps to Successful Selling

Work Smart, Sell Effectively, Make Money

7 Steps to Successful Selling

Work Smart, Sell Effectively, Make Money

Traci Bild

Todd Shafer, Contributing Author

A Perigee Book

A Perigee Book
Published by The Berkley Publishing Group
A division of Penguin Putnam Inc.
375 Hudson Street
New York, New York 10014

Copyright © 2001 by Traci Bild and Todd Shafer
Text design by Tiffany Kukec
Cover design by Liz Sheehan

First edition: August 2001
Published simultaneously in Canada.

Visit our website at
http://www.penguinputnam.com

Library of Congress Cataloging-in-Publication Data
Bild, Traci.
7 steps to successful selling : work smart, sell effectively, make money / Traci
Bild; Todd Shafer, contributing author.
p. cm.
ISBN 0-399-52687-0
1. Selling. I. Title: Seven steps to successful selling. II. Shafer, Todd.
III. Title.
HF5438.25 .B53 2001
658.85—dc21   2001016314

Printed in the United States of America

10 9 8 7 6 5 4

*For my mother, Brittney, who gave me the wings to fly
and to my husband, David, who taught me how to use them.*

Contents

Acknowledgments

I would first like to thank Todd Shafer, my beloved brother and onetime business partner, who has contributed much of his time and effort to creating the training philosophies outlined in this book. I would also like to express my greatest appreciation to those family members and friends who have supported my dream and encouraged me to persist despite all obstacles. Thanks to my husband, David, who put up with the long hours, travel, and time spent on this book. Thanks to my mother, Brittney Blauser, who encouraged me to dream big. To my father, Robert Shafer, and his wife, Trudy: your belief in me has been unshakable, thank you. I would also like to thank Troy and Gabrielle Shafer for all your prayers and Geoffrey and Patricia Bild. Thank you all for your encouragement and unconditional love. A big thank-you goes to all my seminar attendees, who have helped make the system taught in this book rock solid. Without your commitment to this training, your constant feedback and belief in me, this book would not have realized fruition. Last but not least, I would like to thank God, my creator, for the guidance, strength, and insight to make all things possible, including this book.

7 Steps to Successful Selling

Work Smart, Sell Effectively, Make Money

The Road to Sales Success

Corporate America is beginning to feel the sting of employees' discontentment with long hours, conformity, and little appreciation. Workers want financial independence and a lifestyle that provides freedom, innovation, recognition, and fun. Living the life of a home-based business owner or sales professional promises these rewards and more. The possibilities of freedom and flexibility are priceless.

Though many people eagerly enter the sales profession or start a business of their own, not everyone has the experience to build a successful business or succeed in sales. Many people who start a business in their home have little prior experience, yet the rewards make the risk worth taking. Because of a risk I decided to take several years ago, I am living a life that I once only dreamed of. I was in retail management, putting myself through college. Each year just twelve managers out of

350 nationwide were picked and rewarded for overall store performance. I won this prestigious award in my first year of management. You could say I had my career path all plotted out to continue to manage a successful store, be promoted to upper-level management, and hopefully one day run the company. I was on the right path and I knew I could do it. Then one day I received a telephone call from my mother. She had started a janitorial service several years prior and was beginning to get overwhelmed by the day-to-day trials the business presented. She told me that she was going to sell the business and move on to something more enjoyable. I don't know whether it was out of loyalty to my mother or just what life had destined for me, but I resigned from my job and moved back home to help my mother build her business.

A year later, I found myself knee-deep in toilets, scrubbing and waxing floors, cleaning windows, and on the verge of burnout. We had grown the business from three employees to sixty, had annual contracts for over $500,000 in corporate accounts, and had no idea how to manage it all. As they say, life gives the test first, then the lesson. Several years after owning our corporate janitorial service, we decided to sell and move on to bigger and better things that we enjoyed. Free of owning my business, I went back to accomplish the dream I had previously pursued, to run a successful retail conglomerate. I interviewed with the same company, was offered twice the salary I had before, and began right where I had left off. This time something was different. I no longer had the passion that I once had. I did not like working for a *paycheck,* and I no longer had any drive. Owning my own business had opened my eyes to something unexpected—*freedom.* I immediately longed for the flexible schedule that I had taken for granted, the freedom to make decisions, and to take risks.

Again, I resigned. This time I made a promise to myself that I would find a business or a career in sales that provided all the benefits of my first business yet was something that I loved and that utilized my natural talents and abilities. It took some time, but life was carving a place for me. I committed to never work a *job* again. Then, after searching and committing to settling for only the best, I made my mark. I started a company with my brother, Todd, and we brought the first ever sales-driven day planner to the market, the *Sales Success Planner*™. Word spread, sales soared, and an innovative training program was born. Due to the planner, people in sales and home-based business could immediately identify their strengths and weaknesses, and they called us looking for solutions—which we provided. Before I knew it, my brother and I were speaking nationally, changing lives, and helping people to work smart, not hard, so they could work less and make more. Eventually Todd and I decided to pursue our own career paths and I started my current company, Dynamic Performance; offering innovative and affordable training solutions for companies looking to maximize the performance of their sales force both personally and professionally (it is my belief that one has impact on the other).

I have worked with a wide range of business owners—from part-time stay-at-home moms to corporate executives. Whatever your experience level, this book provides the processes and tools to ensure your success, not only financially but in all areas of life. Use them consistently to make miracles happen. My mission is simple: I help sales professionals and home-based business owners reach their desired level of income and maintain or exceed that income, all while learning to work less and make more.

Why do I target these markets? For these reasons:

- A sales- or home-based business opportunity is available to everyone regardless of education, experience, know-how, talents, race, creed, or color.

- Sales- and home-based businesses offer unlimited potential for financial and personal growth.

- The sales profession and home-based businesses help keep families together because they allow us to have more time at home; a key ingredient to building successful relationships with spouses, children, and friends.

■ Sales- and home-based businesses support hopes and dreams of change for the better.

The sales profession is one of the oldest and greatest professions in America. The opportunities are endless and home-based businesses are rapidly becoming the wave of the future due to the freedom and unlimited potential they can provide for individuals and families and for you, too. Using the integrated steps presented in this book will make that unlimited potential real.

Through much trial and error, much listening and problem solving, I have perfected a system that will produce a level of income guaranteed to take you beyond your wildest dreams. This successful system is based on what sales professionals call production. And experience has taught me one basic truth: the activities that create production are calling and seeing prospects, nothing more. This book explains what that basic truth means to you. *7 Steps to Successful Selling* is dedicated to helping you master the activities that promote production, so you can achieve the ultimate in sales success.

How have I helped home-based business owners and sales professionals consistently make calling and seeing prospects their primary focus? By providing them with a step-by-step system that does not just tell them *what* to do, but *how* to do it. This book will provide you with the nuts and bolts to build a thriving business or sales career.

The steps are:

1. Calling 101

2. Appointments 101

3. Finding Needs

4. Producing Activity

5. Tracking Activity

6. Formula for Success

7. Prospecting

Utilizing these steps will:

- Keep you focused on the activities that promote production.

- Act as a system for personal accountability.

- Create consistency in your business.

- Quickly build effective communication skills.

- Provide the answer to "What amount of work is required of me to accomplish my desired financial goal?"

7 Steps to Successful Selling's step-by-step training system encompasses all of these areas. It is important to note that each aspect of the training is effective only when all steps are implemented. Specifically, 7 *Steps to Successful Selling* outlines a process guaranteed to get you in front of qualified prospects. It illuminates a method to put prospects at ease during appointments. It shows how to effectively communicate with people both on the telephone and in person. And it explains how to use the tools that promote production: Activity Management, the Activity Point System, and the Formula for Success in full detail. This book is all you need. By using it, you will experience for yourself how the philosophies presented are commonsense simple. The concepts and techniques, when put into action, will fuel your success because they emphasize what matters most: calling people and seeing prospects.

Calling 101

The telephone. It is a technological wonder that has made the possibilities of financial success readily available to everyone. Anyone with a product or service can contact thousands of potential prospects using a telephone. It puts the world you want to reach at your fingertips. Making contacts is the key to successfully growing your business or improving your sales production. Your telephone is the most effective way to make contacts and it is easy to use. So if you have difficulty achieving your desired level of success, improve your use of the telephone. This alone will help you jump over hurdles quickly. Sales professionals oftentimes face this invisible barrier, picking up the telephone, when beginning their workday. There is temptation to run one more errand, answer one more e-mail, and deal with one more distraction.

According to sales experts, 84 percent of all sales

professionals have call reluctance and fear of the telephone. As a sales professional, you probably know that
no magical telephone scripts will remove your fear. No
script can assure you of 100 percent success on the
telephone. However, you can enhance your communication skills and improve your understanding of how to
control conversations. You can become a true telephone
professional. By applying the concepts and techniques
explained in this chapter, you will not only get results
easily and become a telephone pro, you will see a big
difference in your profits.

Characteristics of a Telephone Professional

In this chapter, we will introduce the characteristics
of a telephone professional and explain what each means
to you. A telephone professional does the following:

- Makes calls during **prime calling times**

- Overcomes call reluctance and fear of the telephone

- Controls the telephone conversation

- Understands and uses **controlled** responses

- Knows the difference between **approach calling,
  service calling,** and **appointment calling**

- Works to steadily improve telephone skills

■ Sets one appointment for every second contact or better

Telephone pros get the appointments that lead to sales. Yet most sales professionals fail to reap the fruits of their efforts because they call without regularity or strategic organization. They often *wing it* without fully understanding how people communicate. A telephone pro, on the other hand, keeps control of the call. They understand that when *winging it,* there is a risk of handing over much of that control to the prospect.

Is call reluctance and fear of the telephone keeping you from achieving great success?

Consider how you currently approach telephone conversations: Doyoutalkquicklytosomeoneonthephonewho cannotgettotalkatallbecauseyou'retalking? You can hardly call that one-sided, breathless approach a conversation. Instead, make sure to set up a real dialogue. Approach each telephone conversation using a simple five-step process. You will discover it is like mastering the scales on a musical instrument: techniques learned when practicing the musical scales improve your playing ability. The five steps are like scales: practicing them will make calling people flow more smoothly.

I recently received an e-mail from Fran, who is in network marketing. Fran had attended one of my seminars and, after two months of using the techniques learned, wrote to say that the seminar had changed her life. Fran had no problems talking with people face-to-face, but felt she was ineffective on the telephone. This, in turn, made it difficult for her to make the calls that are the lifeline of any network marketing business. Fran said, "I always knew the objective was to get the appointment, but I had a pretty high failure rate!"

After implementing the process you are about to learn, Fran's productivity on the telephone skyrocketed. In the first month of using it she booked more appointments and signed up more recruits than in any other month since first starting her business. She contributed the difference to knowing what to expect when talking with prospects on the telephone. Fran now knows what she is going to say, and how the prospect is going to respond, because she has a process in place. She now has control of the conversation and where it's going instead of the other way around. Fran's efforts to become more effective in her business paid off: she was promoted and moved into an entirely new income bracket!

The Five-Step Process

Applying the five-step process can do wonders for your telephone success for three reasons:

- It prevents prospects from being guarded and resistant by disarming them.

- It shows you care about what is important to them.

- You learn to eliminate fear of the telephone and fear of rejection by increasing your understanding of how people communicate.

Becoming completely familiar with this process will allow you to gain sophistication and confidence when making sales calls. Most importantly, you will find ways to sincerely help people. Please realize that the process presented here is not, in and of itself, a shortcut to becoming a telephone professional. To obtain the best results, learn the purpose of each step and the theory behind its purpose. With practice, you will determine the best choice of words for different situations and become comfortable when using them. You will have greater success when calling people by understanding the objectives, purpose, and applications of each step within the process. These steps are:

1. The Opening

2. Disarming

3. The Reason

4. Checkmate Question

5. Checkmate Close

On the telephone, your desired result is to get appointments. By staying committed to this process, you will get all the appointments you want . . . and discover how miracles happen. Do not change or quit if you have a few bad experiences. Instead, reflect on difficult conversations and ask yourself, *how well did I work toward accomplishing each objective at each step? What needs to happen differently?* Doing this requires you to be aware of your tone of voice and attitude at all times while on the telephone. Since the people you are speaking with cannot see you, their impressions will be made by the way you present yourself on the telephone. Focus on mastering the details of each step and notice what works for you and what does not. I suggest setting a small tape recorder next to your telephone so that you can listen to each call and perfect each step.

> *Remember, you control your successes and failures.*
> *So get focused and committed . . . and expect miracles.*

Before going to the first step, confirm that you have the right person on the telephone. Simply saying, "Hello, may I speak with _____" gets you started. Once you know you are talking to the person you want, proceed.

1. THE OPENING

In this first step, your objective is to get a **simple acknowledgment**. This will be accomplished more easily when you have a good attitude and use a friendly tone of voice.

Getting a simple response plays a critical role in succeeding because you want the prospect to get involved in the conversation . . . slowly but surely. Remember, you want to elicit a very simple response like:

- "Yes."
- "Who?"
- "Hello."
- "How are you?"
- "Do I know you?"

Start with this opening statement:

"Hello, (their first name). This is (your name) calling."

Be sure to say both your first and last names. Do not state your company's name at this point, but do address each prospect by using his or her first name only. If you do not know their first name, make an approach call and find out what it is. You might say, "I would like to send Mr. Jones some information on my services and I wondered if you could tell me his first name?" This approach allows you to obtain the information necessary to make your call to Mr. Jones personal. When using the person's last name, it signals that you are prospecting and can quickly set up feelings of resistance.

When starting your conversation with an Opening step such as, "Hi John, this is Traci Bild calling," 99 percent of prospects will respond by saying "yes." It is important to obtain a yes response because this means the prospect has provided an affirmative reply. This type of reply immediately puts the prospect in a positive state of mind. Your goal is to get five "yes" responses in the first 60 seconds of each conversation, and the first yes typically comes from the Opening.

If your prospect asks "Who?" simply repeat your name and pause until hearing a yes. If the response is "Do I know you?" simply say "No, you don't" and move on to the next step, Disarming. If the person says, "How are you?" reply briefly, and then quickly move into the Disarming step. Practice helps you avoid getting flustered.

There is magic in the word Calling

You will find there is magic in the word *calling*, it is like wrapping a special ribbon around your name. "Calling" instantly builds curiosity. This works to your advantage because curiosity generally yields positive responses. In turn, positive responses are key to creating a positive telephone experience. Repeated positive experiences not only increase your odds of getting appointments, they keep you in a positive frame of mind even when you are not getting appointments. Overall, they make it easier to pick up the telephone again and keep calling people so you can be seeing people. Using the word *calling* also adds an aura of confidence and prestige. This again works to your advantage because it sets up a positive atmosphere and experience.

Create a Positive Atmosphere

Check your attitude before picking up the telephone. If you feel down or negative, postpone your calling. Conveying an upbeat attitude is everything . . . and anyone who picks up the telephone will catch on to negativity immediately. Mirroring your prospect's telephone manner aids communication. If you are talking with someone who is high-energy, speed up the way you talk. If he or she comes across in a mellow way, slide your energy level down. This also helps you control the conversation. Having a caring tone in your voice is key. It helps you engage in conversation and instantly creates the positive atmosphere you want.

Build Curiosity

Build a sense of curiosity in your conversation. When those you call wonder who you are, you have their attention. They are listening. Be sure to listen when they talk and notice if they listen when you talk. Then, and only then, does conversation take place. Often, telemarketers working for large firms refuse to leave an opening in their scripts for the call recipient to speak. That simply defeats the purpose of their telephone call. Remember, when you listen to your prospects and know they are listening to you, you are communicating. So open the telephone call with every new prospect using this phrase:

> Hello (prospect's first name), this is (your first and last name) calling.

Then *pause*. Wait as long as necessary until you get a response.

Your objective is to get a response. Wait for it, then go on to the next step, Disarming.

> *The right word may be effective, but no word was ever as effective as a rightly timed pause.*
> —MARK TWAIN

2. DISARMING

In this second step your objectives are to:

- Get a "yes" response

- Obtain permission to talk

In this era of frequent telemarketing calls, it has become second nature for people to resist telephone solicitation. Resistance can be lowered or eliminated by getting the people you call to say yes early in the conversation. This creates a positive atmosphere and opens lines of communication. When hearing a yes response, you are increasing the odds of getting permission to talk and obtaining an appointment. Remember, getting permission to talk is the only way to ensure the other person is listening.

How to obtain a yes response in the Disarming step:

Make positive disarming statements. The easiest way to get a yes response is to start this step with one of the following phrases:

I understand . . . or If you recall . . .

If you know something about the person, use "I understand." For example, you might say, "I understand you're a member of the chamber of commerce." If you met the person previously, say "If you recall, we met at the airport yesterday."

Here are some additional examples:

- "I understand you are a good friend of Michele Kohr."

- "I understand you are in charge of media relations."

- "I understand you are the director of education."

- "If you recall, we met briefly at Barnes and Noble yesterday."

- "If you recall, I introduced myself at the chamber meeting last Monday."

- "If you recall, I gave you my business card when we met at the Bucks game Saturday."

You will always get a yes response to one of these statements because you are stating a fact (unless your information is wrong). If you call people listed in a directory or phone book and know nothing about them, it does not make sense to use phrases like "I understand . . ." or "If you recall . . ." In this case, open the conversation as usual, but instead of recalling an event or stating a fact, get permission to talk; the second objective in the Disarming step. The only reason to skip the first part of the Disarming step is if you lack knowledge about the person. Always scan the lead for any information that can be utilized in the Disarming step. For example, if the lead list contains names of new people moving into the Austin area and the lead is two years old, instead of saying "I understand you recently moved into the Austin area," simply say "I understand you live here in the Austin area."

*　　*　　*

Next, ask for permission to continue the conversation. When telemarketers fail to do this, prospects frequently hang up the phone. Most people feel slighted that the caller failed to check in with them before talking and pushing their product. Here are some appropriate ways to ask for permission:

- "Is this a convenient time for you to talk?"

- "Do you have a quick minute?"

- "Did I catch you at a good time?"

When you politely ask one of these timing questions, be prepared to hear one of the following responses:

- "Yes."

- "No."

- "What is this about?"

If they say no, simply reply by asking one of the following questions:

- "Would an hour from now be better?"

- "Would this time tomorrow work better for you?"

- "Would early next week work better for you?"

Typically, if the prospect says this is not a good time to talk, it probably is not. *Do not force the conversation.* Write the agreed-upon time in your day planner or PalmPilot and return the call at that time. Be sure to begin the return call with the Opening step.

Alternatively, if the response is "What's this about?" you now have permission to move into the Reason step. If asked to call back at a more convenient time, Disarm your prospect when you make your future call by saying, "If you recall, we spoke briefly an hour ago (or yesterday or last week)." Wait for a yes response, then say "Is this a better time for you?" Again, wait for a yes response.

Prospects typically say yes when asked for permission to talk. Ironically, these same people usually put up their guard when telemarketers call. When using these ideas, it will become evident that prospects never become guarded when permission to talk is obtained prior to moving forward. Prospects appreciate the respect granted them and psychologically they become Disarmed in the first two steps.

Here is a quick review before going on to the third step:

1. The Opening

To go from the *Opening* step to the *Disarming* step, be sure to get a simple, positive response, which starts a meaningful dialogue.

"Hello _____, this is _____ calling (pause)."

Upon receiving your simple response of "yes", "who", or "do I know you?" move on to step two.

2. Disarming

I understand . . . or if you recall . . .

"I understand you are a physician at St. Mary's Hospital."
"I understand you are a good friend of David Jones."
"If you recall, we met at the Performing Arts Center last Friday."

After the yes response, ask for permission to talk by saying:

"Is this a convenient time for you to talk?"
"Do you have a minute?"
"Did I catch you at a good time?"

If yes, go on to step three. If no, ask:

"Would an hour from now be better?"

If yes, call back in an hour. Repeat the Opening step and then go to the Disarming step by saying:

"If you recall, we spoke about an hour ago."

Wait and expect a yes response. Then ask for permission to talk by saying:

"Is this a better time for you?"

If you hear a yes response, go to the next step, the Reason. By controlling the conversation to this point, you have obtained three yes responses. As you go on to the Reason step, your prospect has engaged in a dialogue and probably feels comfortable with you. This alone makes him or her more receptive to what you have to say. Now we are ready for the third step.

3. THE REASON

In this third step your objective is to:

- Obtain an *appointment* or an *objection*
- Name the company you are with
- Explain the purpose of your call
- Be very personable, be caring, be yourself

■ Seek controlled, predictable responses

■ Use warm words like visit, get acquainted, hoping, wondering, trying, help, need

Always start this step with the following statement:

"The reason I'm calling is because . . ."

End this step with an **optional close**. This means you give the prospect a choice of two (morning or afternoon), not a choice of yes or no:

"I was wondering if weekdays or weekends work better for you?"

or

"I was wondering if early mornings or afternoons work better for you?"

or

"I'm scheduling appointments for the next four weeks and I was wondering what works better for you, _____ or _____?"

or

"I have gift baskets from $10 to $50 and I was wondering what price in that range would work best for you?"

or

"I just wanted to do a quick service call to ensure you do not need anything. Do you have a minute to answer a few questions or would you prefer to schedule a time to visit together?"

or

"I would really like an opportunity to visit with you for just 15 to 20 minutes and I was wondering if _____ or _____ works better for you?"

or

"I work with a number of _____ here in the _____ area and I was hoping to visit with you for 15 to 20 minutes. I was wondering if mornings or afternoons were better for you?"

State Your Timeframe

It is important to say "for 15 to 20 minutes" in this step of the telephone conversation. Here is why: when you first talk to prospects, in their minds they do not need your product or service. Therefore, they naturally object to meeting with you. By asking for only 15 to

20 minutes, you understand that, psychologically, people can handle an interruption for this amount of time . . . but no more. Once you meet face-to-face, this timeframe gives you the window to uncover your prospect's needs. That is when they realize for themselves the benefits your product or service brings to their lives.

If you asked for a 45- to 50-minute appointment, how do you think your prospects would react? Most people do not have this much time to spare. In their opinion, other things have more value than meeting with you. So they quickly say no when asked for an appointment. By stating you only need 15 to 20 minutes, there is a better chance of getting in front of them. They will likely make the connection between their needs and your product or service at the appointment. That is when they get more involved. They now see value and a way to solve a problem easily. Be careful not to take this interest for granted. When you see the appointment is going well, be sure to politely ask for more time rather than just taking it. Do not feel intimidated by asking for this short amount of time at first. Experience shows that saying "15 to 20 minutes" gets you in front of more people. And the more people you see, the more you will sell. If you're uncomfortable with scheduling short appointments or find it impossible to accomplish your objective in this short amount of time, simply do not mention the time needed at all (unless they ask).

Master the Details of Your Call

When you begin the Reason step, aim to set up an appointment. If an appointment is booked, remember exactly what you said and repeat it on your next call. Take time to notice and practice all the phrases that work for you. Realize that people are more likely to give an objection than an appointment and keep in mind that overcoming objections does not cause people to book with you, finding a need does. Many people in sales feel that if they can overcome all the objections of their prospect or client then they will be able to book an appointment. You may succeed in overcoming objections and booking the appointment, but the question you have to ask is, "will the appointment hold?" If the prospect is not excited to meet with you, he or she may cancel at the last minute due to the lack of value associated with your meeting. However, if you take the time to identify a need, you in turn create value and people will give you their time. Most people, if made aware of a need, will take action to have it filled. By nature we want solutions to our problems.

I recently received a call from Cheryl, who owns her own business. Cheryl worked diligently to set appointments only to see them canceled at the last minute. She found it difficult to stay motivated and often became frustrated because she couldn't be sure that the appointments set would actually hold. After implementing this telephone process, Cheryl not only increased her call ratio to one out of two, but her holding ratios doubled.

The increase in production was immediate and she committed to never winging her calls again. The process used allowed her to identify the needs of her clients prior to getting together. This in turn created excitement in her prospect's eyes and instead of canceling, he or she anxiously awaited the scheduled meeting date. Additionally, knowing the prospect's needs in advance allowed Cheryl to be more prepared for her appointments, resulting in higher appointment sales.

If in the Reason step you receive an objection instead of the desired appointment, do not fret. The fourth step, the Checkmate Question, will help you to quickly identify the needs of your prospect. For example, if you call Ron, a thirty-five-year-old father of four, to discuss insurance needs, like many other young men, he would probably feel no need to meet with you. In his opinion, he is the picture of good health and will be around for many years to come. However, if you have the skill to identify a need that he might not otherwise know he has, you will succeed in booking an appointment that will hold. If you receive an objection such as, "I don't need to worry about insurance now, call me in about ten years," instead of overcoming the objection, you should say something like, "Ron, if you were in a fatal accident tomorrow, what impact would that have on your family financially?" Ron would probably have concern and realize that a need does indeed exist. When a need is identified, it creates value, and when value is created, people will give you their time. Many people

spend time learning how to respond to various objections with the goal of overcoming them. All this does
is bring the prospect's guard back up. Do not worry
about any objection no matter how difficult it may
seem. From this point forward, when you hear an objection, simply say:

> "I understand. While I have you on the telephone, may
> I ask you one quick question?"

If they say yes, you have accomplished your objective.
You are ready to move on to the next step, the Checkmate Question, where you will determine the prospect's
highest need. Remember, your goal in this step is to
obtain an appointment or an objection, either will do.

Write Down Your Reason

Take time to write down your own reason clearly and
succinctly. When writing your reason down, make sure
it fits your comfort zone yet still meets the objective
to get an appointment or an objection.

Here are some examples of reasons:

> "The reason I'm calling is because I am an agent with
> Northeastern Life and you had expressed an interest in
> learning about our disability policies. I was calling to
> see what time would be best for you to get together—
> mornings or evenings?"

or

"The reason I'm calling is because I am a consultant with Fun Time Advertising here in the San Diego area. I'm currently scheduling my April appointments and I was hoping to visit with you to share a little bit about the services I provide. What would work best for you to get together, mornings or afternoons?"

or

"The reason I'm calling is because I am a consultant with Creative Cosmetics and I am working to grow my business. The only way I know to do this is to call on as many people as I can in hopes of setting up a 15- to 20-minute appointment to share the benefits of my services. I would like the opportunity to visit with you and I was wondering if daytime or evenings work better?"

or

"The reason I'm calling is because I am a representative with Avery Ford and I have been trying to find the time to become acquainted with residents here in the Tampa area. I noticed you showed some interest in the new Mustang convertible. I would like the opportunity to visit with you for about 15 to 20 minutes. I was

wondering, would you prefer to come into the dealer-
ship or have me stop by your home?"

Take a Moment to Write Several of Your Own Reason Steps

The reason I'm calling is because _____

_____

and I wondered what might work best to get together, _____ or _____.

or

The reason I'm calling is because _____

_____

and I wondered what might work best to get together, _____ or _____.

Before moving on to the next step, consider what happens differently when you have not met the prospect
before.

What If You Do Not Know Anything About Your Prospect?

If you make cold calls (which I do not recommend)
and know nothing about your prospect, your goal in
the Reason step is to get permission to ask questions
regarding your product or service. Be sure the questions
you ask are open-ended and designed to identify needs
regarding your product or service.

Here's an example:

> "The reason I'm calling is because I'm a consultant with
> Web Designs and I am working to grow my business,
> and the only way I know to do this is to contact as
> many business owners in the area as I can. I am hoping
> to ask a few brief questions regarding your experience
> or knowledge of commercial websites. If you have a
> minute, would you mind if I asked you just a few
> brief questions?"

If given permission, move on to the Checkmate
Question.

Your objective is to ask good questions so you can
have a meaningful conversation and create a bond. A
good, caring conversation will increase your odds of
getting an appointment with every person called. **This
also works well if you do not go on appointments
at all**. Instead of seeking an appointment, you are seeking permission to ask a few brief questions regarding
your product or service and offering solutions to their
stated needs. These types of questions will be covered
in step two on Finding Needs.

In the game of chess, the rules state that each move
made must be followed by an opponent's move. If an
attempt is made to make two moves in a row, the rules
are broken and the game ends. Likewise, turns must be
taken with your prospect to effectively maneuver
through the five-step telephone process. You move.

They respond. You move. They respond . . . and so on. That means to move on to the next step, you must wait for a response. Symbolically, you are both playing chess.

4. CHECKMATE QUESTION

In this fourth step your objectives are to:

- Uncover a need or motivation

- Care about your prospect's need or motivation

- Listen

Asking questions to uncover a need or motivation makes it clear that you care about what your prospects think and feel. People appreciate this and can tell when interest is sincere. *Remember, people buy based on an identified need or motivation.*

We have worked with some of the following examples. To help you accomplish this objective, start by asking a good question like:

STOCKBROKER:
"What is most important to you in regards to your financial portfolio?"

or

<u>INSURANCE AGENT:</u>

"If you walked out the door today and were in a fatal accident, what impact would that have on your surviving family?"

or

<u>REAL ESTATE AGENT:</u>

"What is most important to you in regards to the home you decide to purchase?"

The Checkmate Question will reveal your prospect's highest need. If they indicate they have no need, ask them another question pertaining to a different product or service you offer. You want to quickly identify their number one need. This identification motivates them to take action. Without pinpointing a need, it is difficult to go to the next step, the Checkmate Close. So pick your questions wisely, ask them with confidence, and listen carefully. The clues lie in the responses to your questions.

Write Down Your Checkmate Questions

Take time to write down a series of questions that would be appropriate for the people you are talking with. Keep these questions handy while on the telephone so you can refer to them as needed.

- _____

- _____

- _____

- _____

Once you have written them down, move on to the next step, the Checkmate Close.

Your objective in this step is to reiterate your prospect's highest need in order to get an appointment or close a sale (if no appointments are necessary). Let him or her know you have experience helping others deal with similar needs. Exude confidence.

5. CHECKMATE CLOSE

In this fifth step, the objectives are to:

- Obtain the appointment (no objections) or close a sale

- Use the word *especially*

- Reiterate your reason for calling

- Repeat the identified need or motivation

In this step be sure to relate to your prospect, listen, and show that you care. Express how you have helped others with similar concerns so that they feel you are

an expert in your particular field. If you are new to
sales then share how your *company* (instead of you) has
helped others with similar concerns. The key to this
final step is relating, understanding, and letting them
know you have a solution. Do not state what the solution is. If your goal is to set an appointment, save the
solution for your meeting to ensure it holds. If you do
not go on appointments then this is where you would
share solutions to their stated needs and close the sale.

People take action based on their needs or motivations. Helping your prospects identify their needs and
repeating them in your conversation shows that you care
and have listened to what they just said. In addition,
immediately let them know you have experience in their
areas of concern and that you can be of great service.

Reiterate Your Reason for Calling

Clearly identifying needs and speaking about them
separates you from other competitors who call. This step
leads you to becoming a champion producer. Always
start this step with the following statement:

"_____ (their name) this is one of the reasons I was
hoping to visit with you."

or

"_____ (their name) this is one of the reasons I was
calling (if you do not go on appointments)."

The prospect must feel you called for a specific purpose. The only one they care about is their own particular need. Then, relate to your prospects by letting them know you have worked with a number of people with the same concerns. This puts them at ease. Using the word *especially* allows you to highlight the prospect's need and displays your ability to listen. After relating and repeating the need, let the prospect know you can be of service. Always end this step with a choice of two options for your prospect to choose from, as discussed previously. This is called an Optional Close. For example, if you only want to hold appointments on weekdays, you would say, "What might work best for you, mornings or afternoons?" If you hold appointments only in the evenings and on weekends you would say, "What might work best for us to get together, a weeknight or a weekend?" If you do not go on appointments at all, you might say, "I can send you a packet of information or you can go directly to my website, what might work best for you?" The Checkmate Close is designed to comfort the prospect and help them realize they do need your services. Now that value has been created, the prospect will find a time to speak further or meet with you.

Here are some examples of how to apply the Checkmate Close step:

INSURANCE AGENT:

Your prospect just answered the Checkmate Question: "If you walked out the door today and were in a fatal accident, what impact would that have on your family?"

A: "They would be devastated. I am the bread-winner of the family and there is no way they could continue to live the lifestyle they do today. College education would not be possible either and that concerns me."

Your Checkmate Close response would then be:

"This is one of the reasons I was hoping to visit with you, to share how I've helped other families ensure their quality of life will not be jeopardized due to the untimely death of a major wage earner, *especially* when it comes to providing a college education. I only need 15 to 20 minutes of your time. I'll be in your area Monday afternoon and again on Thursday evening. Which would work better for you?"

or

REAL ESTATE AGENT:

Your prospect just answered the Checkmate Question: "What is currently most important to you in regards to the home you decide to purchase?"

A: "I am looking for a home in a good location and it is imperative the home have the master bedroom positioned away from all other bedrooms."

Your response would be:

"This is one of the reasons I was hoping to have you stop by my office, to share how I've helped other new home buyers find the perfect home, *especially* when it comes to the architecture and layout of the bedrooms. I only need 15 to 20 minutes of your time. Can you stop by this week or would next week work better for you?"

or

STOCKBROKER:

Your prospect just answered the Checkmate Question: "What is most important to you in regards to your financial portfolio?"
A: "I like high-risk stocks that offer a high return. I will not be retiring for another 25 years and would like my money working for me in the meantime."

Your response would be:

"This is one of the reasons I was hoping to speak further with you, to share how I've helped other investors create a strong portfolio, *especially* where high risk and high returns are concerned. I would like to get together with you and share how I helped them. Would you prefer we meet or would you like to discuss how I can help you right now?"

Doing this will take your business to a higher level. By using the Checkmate Close, your prospects can see that you understand their specific needs and have solutions. Stating that you have helped others with similar concerns creates comfort and displays experience. Apply the Checkmate Question and the Checkmate Close steps to improve your telephone contact-to-appointment ratio, which is covered later in this chapter. Your objective is to set appointments with prospects so you can provide solutions to their specific needs. Using all five steps will help you achieve that in as few calls as possible and mastering this telephone process greatly enhances your skills when calling and seeing people. It helps you communicate with ease and empowers your prospects to talk freely with you.

Know the Purpose of Each Call

Not all calls are made to set appointments. Learn the difference between *approach calling, appointment calling,* and *service calling.*

An **approach call** is designed to obtain information regarding a prospect. An **appointment call** is made in hopes of meeting the prospect, while a **service call** is simply a follow-up courtesy call that could bring in additional sales.

If you want to make contact with unknown decision makers in large organizations, make an **approach call**. Here is one way to get by the gatekeeper who answers the phone. Say:

> "I need to fax some information to your company about _____. What is your fax number? And to whom should I address it?"

Actually, it is not necessary to send the fax. You now have a contact name and can call the prospect personally. At that time, you can get permission to send information via mail or fax or, ideally, set an appointment.

An **appointment call** follows when you have just met someone. You would set up an appointment with this person by saying:

> "The reason I'm calling is because you had expressed an interest in _____ and I was calling to see what would work best for you to get together, mornings or afternoons (pause)?"

A **service call** is to build rapport and follow up on a previous conversation by saying:

> "I talked with you about _____ (identify product or service discussed) approximately two months ago. You

had expressed an interest in learning more about _____ and I wondered if you had a minute to answer a few brief questions?"

Write Down Each Step

Once the purpose of each call is determined, state your reason in the Reason step. Ask yourself, *what is my objective with this prospect?* Then apply what you learned in the Reason step. Remember to pause and wait for a response, especially in the Opening step. This pause is strategically placed after your name to initiate the first yes response. It sets the tone of the entire conversation.

Get started by doing the following: Put each telephone step on a different flashcard. When providing training programs, I encourage people to put this telephone process on flashcards so that they are readily available when the time comes to make calls. Write each step on a separate 3-by-5-index card:

1. The Opening
2. Disarming
3. The Reason
4. Checkmate Question
5. Checkmate Close

Then write what you will say in each step on the individual flashcard. Write the word *pause* at the bottom of each card to remind you to wait for a response. Pausing is the key to success in this process. Using this process, rather than a script, keeps focus on what you are trying to accomplish. You are less likely to embarrass yourself with an awkward statement and will create rapport quickly. These successes lead to overcoming any call reluctance and fear of the telephone you feel.

Remember, your success depends on need-based selling, which creates trust and loyalty in your relationships. You sell your products or services to fill a need. So if you are not able to identify your prospect's needs, keep probing. Remain focused on addressing them and their needs, not on you and your product.

Quick Reference

Remember the characteristics of a telephone professional discussed at the beginning of this chapter? Use these points as a reference while practicing the five-step process.

Prime Calling Times

Set aside specific times each week for telephone prospecting so you work smarter, not harder, when setting appointments. Prime Calling Times can only be determined through experimentation. Make prospecting dials at various times on different days and notice when the greatest number of people answer their telephones. Note the beginning and ending call times in your planner or PalmPilot. Trends will emerge, signifying the days and times to designate as your Prime Calling Times. Apply this process to every call session. Determine the key times to make prospecting calls. Yes, this means make an appointment with yourself. This step is that important! Using Prime Calling Times is crucial to the success of your business. I believe firmly that it's not always the mood people are in, but the skill the caller has to engage them in conversation. We have found dinnertime, from 5–7 P.M. to be very successful because people are not sitting around the dinner table eating as a family anymore. Each person will determine their own Prime Calling Time, depending on the habits of their potential clientele.

Jack, who sold life insurance and attended one of my seminars, once told me that he would make prospecting calls every single day. Once he began to track his calling times he realized it was not necessary to call daily and that, quite often, no one was home when he did call. To increase his efficiency, he focused on tracking his calls and the results from those calls for three weeks. At the end of three weeks he looked at the evidence and realized that the best times to call were Tuesdays and Thursdays between the hours of five and seven in the evening! Jack changed his schedule to reflect his new strategy, spent less time on the phone and achieved greater results. He told me that with the free time he created, he started walking his son to school in the mornings and walking him home in the afternoons. Prime Calling Times changed Jack's life and they can change yours, too.

Overcome Call Reluctance and Fear of The Telephone

The dictionary describes *reluctance* as "unwilling; to struggle against" and *fear* as "a state of dread!" You can eliminate both these words from your vocabulary by using the process this book suggests. Your reward is getting one appointment out of every second contact . . . or better. The feeling of success soon will far outweigh any fear and reluctance you may have.

Control the Telephone Conversation

Learn to control the conversation and direct the responses your prospect is most likely to give. This minimizes any uncertainties and surprises.

Understand and Use Controlled Responses

You will become well-practiced in controlling your prospect's responses and aim to elicit yes responses as quickly as possible. Calling 101 keeps you in control of the telephone call. Because controlled responses are being used, it is easy to know what the prospect is going to say before he or she says it. At each step, you know all possible responses. There is nothing you are unprepared for, which means there is nothing to be afraid of (remember Fran's testimony earlier in this chapter?).

Know the Difference Between Approach Calling, Appointment Calling, and Service Calling

Approach Calls: when obtaining information about a prospect, call the receptionist to get a name, address, fax number, etc.

Appointment Calls: when attempting to set up a time to meet a prospect or current customer.

Service Calls: when contact with a prospect or customer has previously been made and you want to follow up to build repeat business.

Set One Appointment for Every Second Contact or Better

When applying and practicing this process, you will obtain one appointment for every two contacts made . . . or better. This is a 2:1 **call ratio**. Calculate your call ratio by dividing the number of contacts made by the number of appointments set up.

Contacts ÷ # Appointments = Call Ratio
e.g., 18 contacts ÷ 9 appointments = 2:1 call ratio

Frequently Asked Questions

Q. How do I get through the secretary or "gatekeeper"?

A. In this situation, when the secretary answers the telephone, state your name prior to asking for the prospect. This keeps the secretary from asking who you are and whom you are with. Typically, he or she will put you right through. Also ask for the prospect by first name only. If he or she asks what the call is regarding, simply say, "It's personal business."

Example: "Hello, this is Jan Smith, is Jack in?"

Q. Do I leave messages?

A. Experience shows that prospects rarely call prospectors back. For this reason, I suggest making three attempts prior to leaving a message. If there is no answer on the fourth attempt, leave a message. However, if an agreed-upon time was set to talk, always leave a message to display your follow-up skills.

With all these characteristics in place, becoming a telephone professional is easily within your reach. Brenda, a professional sales consultant with a Fortune 500 company, recently called our office with overwhelming excitement. Brenda had been with her company for fifteen years and by all accounts was a great success. She was well known in her company, regularly received recognition for high sales, and was a high-income earner. Despite her success, Brenda was overwhelmed by her fear of the telephone. She despised the telephone and always found a reason not to make calls.

When she did make calls, she was semi-effective, but she never enjoyed it.

Brenda decided to do something about her fear and implemented the telephone process you just learned. In one week Brenda completely eliminated her fear of the telephone, her call ratios greatly improved, and her appointments were holding better. Brenda attributed this success to utilizing a process that she could count on to provide consistent results. She felt more comfortable with her prospects because they responded better to her, she quickly identified their individual needs, and was able to share the importance of why an appointment would be beneficial. The best part of the story is Brenda's income increased and her work hours went down. She learned to work her business smarter, not harder, so she could work less and make more.

Appointments 101

Calling 101 taught you to effectively communicate with your prospects using a step-by-step telephone process. As I mentioned, when used, it will lead to obtaining one appointment out of every second contact . . . or better. Once at the appointment, you will want to put prospects into a **Shopper's State of Mind**. *State* is defined as "a condition of mind" and the mind is the part of an individual *that feels, perceives and, especially, reasons.*

When prospects are in a Shopper's State of Mind they become more receptive to discussing your product or service and how it benefits them. You actually help them create a satisfying mental picture . . . they quickly see that your solution can deal with their problem when discussed in the right way. Their state of mind perceives your visit as beneficial, and they begin to mentally *shop* your products or services. The following example will help you understand this concept better:

Frustration Turns to Willingness

Many people resist the idea of saving today for a college education tomorrow. Sometimes families wait and decide to deal with that expense when the time comes; though many set up a savings account ahead of time.

Imagine a middle-class father of four sitting at his desk writing a check he intends to deposit into his daughter's prepaid college fund. Though he is late paying two immediately due bills, he stops to remind himself of the commitment he made to his wife to secure their daughter's education.

This father's current state of mind is one of frustration and anger. He does not see a reward for writing the college fund check immediately, but he would experience instant relief by paying the two critical bills looming on his desk.

Suddenly his daughter walks into the room. She excitedly shows her report card filled with straight A's. He sees the joy in her face and hears the pride in her voice. Instantly, he shifts into a positive state of mind. He suddenly *sees* the benefits of the financial sacrifice he has agreed to make. He stops feeling frustrated. Instead, he feels happy to write a check that leads to his daughter's college education and future happiness.

Did you notice how quickly this father's *state* or *condition of mind* changed? Instantly. In the same way, you can immediately create a picture of value that excites your prospects. Shopper's State of Mind means the prospect is in a state of mind to shop your products or services. You have built immediate excitement and value so that the person you're speaking with suddenly visualizes his or her life as being better because of your products or services, they are shopping in their mind. Engage them in a meaningful conversation about your area of expertise and your odds of success increase greatly . . . especially since you are communicating face-to-face.

People love to be asked their opinions. When they express these opinions, pictures form in their mind. These pictures help them link information to what they already know and care about. When asking for opinions, make sure the questions relate to what *they* care about, not what *you* care about. Often when first meeting a prospect, you feel some tension. Keep in mind this person feels suspicious of you, wondering if you will measure up to the expectations set in your initial telephone call. When you apply Shopper's State of Mind, it is similar to Disarming your prospects on the telephone. You treat them with such respect that resistance simply never comes up. They are immediately open and receptive to what you have to say.

Here is how you put prospects into a Shopper's State of Mind:

1. Ask a question that guarantees a yes response . . . something everyone wants.

Frame your question in a general way. For example:

DIRECT SALES (RECRUITING):
"Is financial freedom important to you?"

or

CONSULTING FIRM:
"Is growing your business important to you?"

or

REAL ESTATE:
"Is working with an agent who understands your needs and expectations important to you?"

2. When they say YES, follow with a question that leads to a description.

DIRECT SALES (RECRUITING):
"What does financial freedom mean to you personally?"

or

CONSULTING FIRM:
"What exactly does growing a business mean to you?"

or

REAL ESTATE AGENT:

"Could you describe what *exceeding* your expectations means to you?"

Let your prospect answer and listen carefully. Realize that each person has a different opinion and a different vision; don't assume everyone has the same mindset. Be patient. The more time it takes to answer a question, the more thinking and reflecting are taking place.

3. Ask for permission to share your ideas.

This step is especially important in building rapport with your prospect. The following examples continue from steps one and two.

DIRECT SALES (RECRUITING):

"May I offer my opinion of what financial freedom means to me?"

or

CONSULTING FIRM:

"May I offer my opinion of what growing a business means to me?"

or

REAL ESTATE AGENT:

"May I offer what exceeding expectations means to me when helping someone purchase a home?"

4. A yes response is your cue to share your mission statement.

Make a statement here that reflects the **mission** of your business. Your mission should demonstrate what you would be able to help the prospect accomplish; it should be passionate and something that helps prospects visualize their lives as being better because of your product or service. For example:

DIRECT SALES (RECRUITING):

"To me, financial freedom means that you are able to reach your desired level of income, maintain that income, then exceed it, all while learning to work less and make more. Would you agree?"

CONSULTING FIRM:

"To me, growing a business means that you are reaching a larger market with your products and services, you are increasing your revenues while lowering your costs, resulting in a higher profit-margin for the company. Would you agree?"

REAL ESTATE AGENT:

"To me, exceeding expectations when purchasing a home means only previewing homes that meet or exceed your requirements, having an agent who sees your vision of what a home should be and who has the ability to negotiate a price that is in your best interest."

Your mission statement must reflect the benefit you bring to your prospects and show how you can make their vision (as they stated in step 2) a reality.

Take time to write your mission statement and commit it to memory. It tells your prospects you can quickly and effectively meet their needs. Explain it easily and with confidence. Take a minute now to create your own mission statement:

_____

_____

_____

The mission statement provides the why *that inspires every* how.

—CHARLES GARFIELD

Shopper's State of Mind is a simple technique that moves your prospects from a suspicious, curious state into an open, focused state. It gets them thinking about their needs and allows you to move into the finding needs phase, which is presented in Step Three. Prospects are now eager to learn how you can help them accomplish their goals. Here is a Shopper's State of Mind example:

Ray, an interior decorator for a large architectural firm, recently told me about his experience with Shopper's State of Mind. He is in a highly competitive market and his skills are vital to the success of his career. Here is how he gets his clients into a Shopper's State of Mind. When first meeting with them he goes through the following process (this example revolves around a client building a new pediatrics center):

"Before we get started, may I ask you just a couple quick questions?"
"Sure."

"Is it important that children and parents visiting your pediatrics center feel comfortable and relaxed?"
"Yes it is."

"In your opinion, what does comfortable and relaxed mean to you, what do you want the children and their parents to feel as they enter your center?"
"I want them to feel as though they have entered a happy place, one that is full of imagination and that helps them create positive

thoughts. My hope is that this will make the children more relaxed prior to meeting with my staff."

"May I share what comfortable and relaxed means to me?"
"Of course!"

"Like you, it means that the children feel safe and that they enjoy being in your center due to the fun, imaginative atmosphere that has been created. It also means that there is a feeling of nostalgia, of home, a place of comfort. We accomplish this by thinking through everything from colors and textures to furniture to help all who visit your center feel at peace and positive about their experience with you."
"You said exactly what I was thinking!"

Ray has found that going through this process puts him several steps ahead of his competitors because it has his potential new clients already shopping his service. While his competitors enter the appointment prepared to tell potential clients what they think should be done, Ray first takes a moment to engage his client in conversation and learn about their decor needs and the impact it will make on their visitors. They form a bond and understand what one expects of the other. Not only is he able to share his mission, he also first incorporates what his client's vision is and wraps it into his mission statement. You can get more ideas about designing your own Shopper's State of Mind process by following the steps shown in this next example. Jeremy sells boats for the number one dealer in the country.

1. Ask a general question, something everyone wants, such as:

"Is leisure and fun important to you?"

2. If the prospect answers yes, then say:

"Can you tell me what you categorize as leisure and fun?"

3. Listen carefully to what they tell you, then say:

"May I offer what fun and leisure means to me?"

4. With your prospect's permission, say how you can benefit her by sharing your own mission statement. Be sure to tie her opinion in too:

Leisure and fun means that you are able to get away from work, leave it at the office, and do something you really enjoy, such as boating. Fun means being able to choose which toy you want to play with on your day off; your water skis, knee board, do you want to fish today, or take the boat to an eat-in marina. Leisure and fun are what boating is all about, would you agree?"

The goal is to get the prospects to see themselves and their families enjoying boating and its benefits before they have made a purchase. Now write your own Shopper's State of Mind process. Paint a picture, just as we did in the interior design and boating examples. Your objective is to move your prospects from a curious, suspicious state of mind into an open and receptive state of mind . . . one that leads to a new awareness of the needs they have.

Take a Moment to Write Your Own Shopper's State of Mind

1. Is _____ important to you?

2. What exactly does _____ mean to you?

3. Can I share what it means to me?

4. (Share your mission):

_____

_____

_____

Finding Needs

While at your appointment, you have just successfully engaged your prospect into being open, focused and receptive: a Shopper's State of Mind. Now your objective is to uncover needs, desires, frustrations, and motivations. Seek to learn more about your prospects and to understand their habits, beliefs, and values. Once you know them better, you can more easily talk about what is important to them, not what's important to you. To do this, complete a **Customer Profile** sheet.

A Customer Profile sheet is a one-page document used to obtain basic information (such as name, address, phone, e-mail) and to identify the needs of your prospect in order of importance. The Customer Profile sheet must be created by you and typeset on a computer. Once done, it should be used on appointments with new prospects and over the telephone or face-to-face with current clients to generate new sales.

Finding Needs simply means asking questions to determine what your client or prospect *needs* in regards to your products or services. Most sales professionals want to first show available products: a show-and-tell approach. They feel this will give them more control over the sale because the prospect does very little talking. Does a show-and-tell approach put prospects into a predetermined category? Yes. Many people in sales attempt to predetermine what products or service their prospects need, what they can afford, and make assumptions that cost them sales. They categorize potential buyers in their minds and mentally determine what the buyer's needs may be. Let's use a car salesman as an example.

A car salesman has a noon appointment with a successful attorney. Because of the attorney's status and income the salesman assumes that the attorney wants to spend top dollar on a car. He has categorized this attorney as a big spender. The salesman is excited and shows him the best cars on the lot, raves about incredible features, and goes on and on about potential upgrades. Mentally, he has the perfect car in mind for his customer and assumes that the attorney is as excited as he is. Meanwhile, the attorney is feeling frustrated and angry that the salesman is showing no interest in what he really needs, which is a four-door car with a great safety record, nothing flashy. His main concern is reliability and protecting his family in the event of an accident. In this case, no sale will be made and both people involved will go away disappointed.

The fact is the lost sale could have been prevented. Knowledge is power and the more you know about your prospect, the more control you will have. To maximize each sale, it is imperative you take the time to reveal needs. This information in turn creates value as you then describe how you may provide solutions to your prospect's identified needs. The Customer Profile sheet may be done in person or over the telephone. By filling out a Customer Profile sheet on your prospect, you avoid making assumptions that could destroy rapport and lose sales. When you truly meet an identified (not assumed) need, your prospects come back to fill future needs. To uncover needs and record the prospects' responses, create a custom Customer Profile sheet. When creating the list of questions that you want to ask your prospects, try to limit all questions to one page. Make multiple copies and use the same Customer Profile sheet on each prospective client. It will give you:

- Predetermined questions to ask, allowing needs to be revealed smoothly

- Detailed information so you can make appropriate recommendations to meet their needs

- Additional pertinent information that leads to future sales

Before asking questions, it is important to obtain permission from your prospect. Here's an example of a Customer Profile sheet that the salesman in the above example could have used to identify the needs of his potential car buyer:

"Before I take you onto the lot to look at cars, may I ask you a few brief questions?" Then, with pen in hand, he would ask the questions and briefly document on the Customer Profile sheet the responses given:

Name: _____

Address: _____

City/St/Zip: _____

Home Phone: _____

Work Phone: _____

E-mail: _____

Can you receive calls at work? Y/N

"Why are you trading in your old vehicle?"
"It has over 150,000 miles on it and it is starting to cost me a lot of money in repairs."

"What is most important to you regarding the purchase of a new car—price, safety, reliability?"
"I would say safety first and price second. I don't like to waste a lot of money on cars because they depreciate so fast."

"What features are you looking for?"
"I am looking for a four-door car that has folding backseats because my wife is a painter and she moves her paintings from gallery to gallery. I also would like electric windows and keyless entry."

"Is there a particular price range you would like to stay in?"
"I would like to stay in the low thirties."

"What other cars are you looking at and why?"
"I am also looking at Saturn because of their great safety record and affordable prices."

"How many cars do you own?"
"We have two."

"How often do you trade these cars in?"
"I would say we trade them about every four years."

Comments: _____

_____

_____

After identifying needs, it is important to repeat them back to your prospect. This shows that you listened and confirms that you heard correctly. For example, the car salesman might say, "Based on what you just told me, it seems that you are trading in your current car because it has a lot of miles and is draining you financially. What is most important to you regarding the purchase of a new car is that it is safe and affordable. The features you are looking for are folding backseats, electric windows, and keyless entry is that correct?" The prospect would then respond by saying yes.

Now, because it is clear what the prospect wants, the salesman can take him to look at cars that fit his specific needs. After closing the sale, the salesman should put the Customer Profile in his files and log in his planner or PalmPilot the next follow-up date. He can also count on another sale from this new client four years from now if he remains in contact because the attorney made it clear that he trades his cars in every four years. The salesman can even go further by asking when they expect to trade in their other car. When the time comes to do the trade, he would want to do a completely new Customer Profile sheet to ensure no assumptions are made and that needs are met.

Creating Your Own Customer Profile Sheet

Your goal is to establish rapport with prospects and gather information to determine if your products or services meet their needs. The Customer Profile sheet is the tool that helps you accomplish this goal and even works to generate future sales with the same client. When creating your own Customer Profile sheet the first few questions asked should be general and appear nonthreatening. As your prospects become more comfortable with you, ask questions that are more detailed so you can recommend specific solutions to their stated needs. Then, repeat the specific needs of your prospects or clients back so they know you listened. This also helps create value as they begin to realize you care about what is important to them. Lastly, offer recommendations that are designed to provide solutions to their stated needs or concerns.

Words are powerful. Choose them carefully and organize your thoughts before you speak. Creating and utilizing a Customer Profile sheet will help you to determine which words best communicate the message you want to send. Attempt to speak in the prospect's language, rather than your own. Only focus on issues that are important to them, not you. Lee Iacocca once said, *"It's important to talk to people in their own language. If you do it well, they'll say, 'God, he said exactly what I was thinking.' And when they begin to respect you, they'll follow you to the death."* Here is a Customer Profile sheet used by our company to find the needs of seminar attendees. We start first with Shopper's State of Mind, and then move into asking questions. To get the full effect, you may want to fill this out yourself.

PERSONAL INFORMATION

Name: _____

Address: _____

City/St/Zip: _____

Home Phone: _____

Work Phone: _____

E-mail: _____

Can you receive calls at work? Y/N

SHOPPER'S STATE OF MIND

1. Is experiencing great success in growing your business important to you? Y/N

2. Can you define what great success in growing your business means to you?

3. Can I share what great success in growing a business means to me? Y/N

4. To me, experiencing great success in growing a business means that you are able to reach your desired level of income, maintain it, then exceed it, all while learning to work less and make more.

FINDING NEEDS

After applying Shopper's State of Mind, we obtain permission to ask a few more questions.

"How long have you been in sales?"

"What do you like most about being in sales?"

"What would you say has contributed most to your success up to this point?"

"What is your long-term goal?"

"What is your desired level of income?"

"Have you been successful in achieving this level of income?"

"In your opinion, what is the biggest challenge you face that keeps you from achieving your desired level of income?"

"What steps or actions have you taken to overcome this challenge?"

"If you were able to eliminate this challenge or road-block from your life right now, what impact would that have on your career?"

APPLYING SOLUTIONS

You will see that by asking questions, you immediately get confirmation that a need does exist. When you repeat these needs back to the prospects in order of importance, your prospects will begin visualizing their lives better because of your product or service. Asking key questions actually helps your prospects identify needs they never realized they had. This is customer service at its best.

These skills can be used to move your customers through your entire product line. Remind yourself that once they become aware of a need, if they don't buy from you, they will buy elsewhere—you can be sure of that. That is why it is important to build your business by asking good questions. Finding needs means determining what your prospect needs in regards to your product or service so you may provide a solution and relief. This requires asking really good questions in hopes of revealing relevant information. Here are some suggestions for starting your dialogue with a Customer Profile sheet that may be used by you. Simply fill in the blanks with questions that are relevant to your industry. Feel free to expand upon these questions, but try to keep them confined to one page.

Do you feel it is important that _____?

What challenges are you facing in _____?

If there were one thing you could change about your current _____ what would it be?

What type of _____ do you currently use?

Do you have any special _____ needs I should know about?

How familiar are you with _____?

How often do you buy _____ products or services?

What is your biggest concern in regards to _____?

What would happen if you were to _____?

Before going to the next chapter, take time to create a Customer Profile sheet that you can use to increase production. At the top of your sheet you want to ask for basic information. Next is Shopper's State of Mind, and, lastly, a minimum of four or five questions to identify needs. You may want to put a comment section at the bottom so that you can note what happened. Your objective is to continue to grow your business by finding and filling the needs of your clients and prospects. Finding needs will create new clients and allow you to expand your product line with the current clients you already serve.

HOW MUCH DOES THIS COST?
THE INEVITABLE QUESTION

When prospects' needs are revealed and solutions are applied, they will be less concerned about price. We live in a society of instant gratification. People want solutions and they want them now. If a prospect is concerned about the price, he or she probably does not see the value your product or service provides. Finding needs reduces the odds of this happening. Your job as a sales professional is to find needs and fill them. It is as simple as that. After reiterating your prospect's needs and offering solid solutions, simply say, "Do you see any reason why we should not get started today?" If your prospect is unable to make the investment necessary to meet all needs disclosed, start with the highest need first and fill it. Then, keep going on to other needs in order of importance. Your prospect will tell you when to stop.

Any needs that are left on the table must be filled over the course of the next twelve months. Use this to your advantage and contact your client, regularly working together until all needs have been met. Your customer will rave about your service and refer you to friends and business associates. Trust has been established and your client will be with you for life.

The sales consultant had an uneasy feeling about the appointment he had set up with Mrs. Evans, whom he had just met briefly. The woman begrudgingly allowed him five minutes of her time if he would come at a specific hour and arrive on time. He rang the doorbell and was greeted with icy resistance. The woman gruffly explained she had been ill with a cold and was recovering from the flu. When he politely started a dialogue by asking, "What does good health mean to you, Mrs. Evans?" he hit a

nerve. She immediately expressed her agony with the
doctors and the medicines they prescribe. She simply
wanted to get stronger so she could fight the germs
that come around. By asking a number of probing
questions, the sales professional pinpointed other
frustrations and offered a solution . . . a selection of
quality vitamins to build her immune system. The
clock, forgotten in the lively discussion, marched on.
More than an hour after he had arrived, Mrs. Evans
said her good-byes and added plenty of thank-yous.
He had made her aware of alternatives to medicine
that would benefit her in the long run . . . and felt
proud to provide a solution to a new customer's need.

Producing Activity

Where performance is measured, performance is improved. In sales, performance refers to activity. The dictionary defines *activity* as "the quality or state of being active." Only when an individual in sales is active will he or she achieve great financial success.

However, the definition of activity must be further clarified. Great success in sales does not come from just any activity, it is only derived from what we call Income Producing Activities. These are the activities that directly impact your bottom line: calling and seeing prospects. And this step will help you focus on producing activity.

Many people have difficulty distinguishing which activities will grow their business. Since most are accustomed to being paid in the form of wages—payment for work performed—we tend to associate *time* with *pay*. The more hours worked, the more money made.

One of sales greatest deceptions is time. Remember, in sales we are not paid for our time, we are paid for our Income Producing Activities. Wealth in any home-based business or sales profession is created from commissions earned, not hours worked. Many people have a difficult time making the transition from wage to commission. Commissions are not based on pay per hour, but on sales made. And as I mentioned, the only activities that lead directly to sales are calling and seeing people. Because of this deception between wage and commission, my company, Dynamic Performance, created the world's only planner designed to help salespeople plan their success: The *Sales Success Planner*.

People don't plan to fail, they fail to plan.

The Sales Success Planner™

The *Sales Success Planner* provides the plan or blueprint for your sales success. Even if you do not choose to use this specific planner, it is still critical that you learn the concepts behind the planner and that you try to implement them into your sales career. People are in search of better time management solutions and the statistics show the magnitude of the problem. The average person owns five to seven planners (*owns* not *uses*) and looks at the one being used ten to twelve times per day. People in sales switch planners regularly because they have difficulty finding a system that works for them. The *Sales Success Planner* is similar to other planners available today except the concepts are different. Most planners are designed to help people plan, organize, and prioritize their day. Our planner's primary focus revolves around activity. The *Sales Success Planner* works in three ways:

- In its most basic form, the *Sales Success Planner* produces visual evidence of activity.

- If used at the next level, it helps people to associate activity with production.

- In its highest form, the *Sales Success Planner* provides the level of activity necessary to achieve any financial goal.

Sales is the greatest profession in the world. You have the ability to work less and make more than ever before. The *Sales Success Planner* takes the focus off the goal itself and puts it on the activities by which you arrive at the goal.

The *Sales Success Planner* includes five distinct sections, each with a specific purpose. The sections are:

1. Daily Task sheet
2. Call box
3. Appointment box

4. Week End summary

5. Activity Point Totals (to be discussed in Step 5).

Please note that you do not have to use this exact planner to implement the concepts explained in this chapter. You can use a notepad or incorporate the philosophies into the planner you may already be using. On the next page is an example of our *Sales Success Planner*.

1. DAILY TASK SHEET

Because of the freedom home-based business owners and sales professionals have, it sometimes becomes difficult to find a balance between business and personal tasks. Neglecting to address both issues in a timely manner can lead to distractions and cause frustration. Use the Daily Task section to minimize frustration. It provides six spaces to note important things to do (both personal and business) and a Notes section for items of importance. This gives you a constant visual reminder of tasks to do, items to remember, and goals to pursue. Though doing this may seem trivial at first, the list will keep your mind from becoming overwhelmed. It allows you to focus more on running your business in an effective, concise manner.

To use the To Do section of the Daily Tasks sheet, simply list the most important tasks that may interfere with Income Producing Activities: calling and seeing prospects. Whenever a task is completed, mark it off

Left page (top)

MONDAY
APR. 9TH
●✕●✕●✕●✕●✕●✕○○○○○○○○ TOTAL AP *187*
○○○○○○○○○○○○○○ SALES *8*

9° - 16³ COLUMBUS DAY ☑

Prospecting Calls
(Holiday. People Home!)

☐ | 6:00 ☐

Dinner at Moms

TUESDAY
APR. 10TH
○○○○○○○○○○○○○○○○○○○ TOTAL AP *115*
○○○○○○○○○○○○○○○○○ SALES *950*

9:00 226.2212 ☑ | 1:30 ✕

Al Roberts | *Rick + Jane Smith*
100 E. Ave #5 Tpa | *430 Pelican Way*

12:00 412.6183 ✕ | ☐

Rhonda Kohn
413 Lake Place Ct.

WEDNESDAY
APR. 11TH
●✕●✕●●●✕●✕●✕●✕✕✕✕ TOTAL AP *320*
○○○○○○○○○○○○○○○○○ SALES *0*

6 - 7 ☐

Gym! No excuses

☐ | 5° - 7 ☑

Prospecting Calls

©Dynamic Performance International

Right page (top)

DAILY TASKS

*People don't plan
to fail
They fail to plan.*

MONDAY	TUESDAY
TO DO'S	
☐ *Flowers for Mom*	☐ *Pick up Dry Cleaning*
☐	☐ *Call Kim Jones*
☐	☐ *Call Kendra Smith*
☐	☐
☐	☐
☐	☐
NOTES	
Catch up mileage book	
Send thank you notes	
Card for Dave	
WEDNESDAY	**ACTIVITY POINT SYSTEM**
TO DO'S	● Dial ☑ Appt. Held 15
☐ *Do Co. paperwork*	● Contact ☒ Sales Made 50
☐ *Grocery Store*	✕ Appointment Ⓡ Recruit 100
☐	**WEEK-END SUMMARY**
☐	Total Sales $ *1375.00*
☐	Total Activity Points *906*
☐	Call Ratio
NOTES	**DAILY EXPENSES**
Goal: 750 Activity	*Tues $25 gas (100 miles)*
Points!	*Tue $15 lunch*

Left page (bottom)

THURSDAY
APR. 12TH
●✕●✕●✕●✕○○○○○○○○○○○ TOTAL AP *284*
○○○○○○○○○○○○○○○○ SALES *425*

9:00 286.8333 ☑ | 12:00 889.2188 ✕

Ayme Hicks | *Telephone Appt.*
828 Cross St. | *Bill Rice*

10⁰⁰ (cell) 493.1430 ✕ | 7:00 ☑

Chris Clark | *Ryans School Dinner*
Meet @ Starbucks

FRIDAY
APR. 13TH
○○○○○○○○○○○○○○○○○○○ TOTAL AP
○○○○○○○○○○○○○○○○○ SALES

GOOD FRIDAY ☐

12:00 ☑ | ☐

Lunch Victoria

2:00 ☑ | ☐

massage!

SAT.
APR. 14TH ○○○○○○○ TOTAL AP
○○○○○○○ SALES

SUN.
APR. 15TH ○○○○○○○ TOTAL AP
○○○○○○○ SALES   EASTER

1:00 ☑ | ☐

Family Photos

©Dynamic Performance International

Right page (bottom)

DAILY TASKS

*People don't plan
to fail
They fail to plan.*

THURSDAY	FRIDAY
TO DO'S	
☐ *Disney World!*	☐ *Call Kari Smith*
☐ *Bring Camera*	☐ *Update files*
☐ *3 Rolls film*	☐ *Train Jackie*
☐ *Snacks*	☐
☐ *Jackets*	☐
☐	☐
NOTES	
• *Call Accountant @*	
Qtly taxes	
• *Pick up copies*	
SATURDAY	**SUNDAY**
TO DO'S	
☐ *2ⁿᵈ B-Day Gift Kelly*	☐ *Cat Show ? 3:00*
☐ *Clean House!*	☐
☐	☐
☐	☐
☐	☐
NOTES	
Send pictures out	*B-Day present Ryan*
Balance Check Book	

on the box at the left. At the end of each week, write any task that is not complete in the To Do section for a specific day the following week so it is not forgotten.

If you work in a focused, concise manner, you will experience success faster than if you spend the same time noodling with no specific direction.

2. CALL BOX

The Call box produces evidence of calls made and reveals the effectiveness of your telephoning skills.

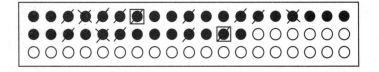

Each circle in the Call box represents one call. Each time a call is made, fill in one circle regardless of what occurred. If a prospect is reached and permission to talk is obtained, put a slash through the filled-in circle. If an appointment is set, add another slash to make an X. See the example below.

● = Dial

◐ = Made a contact

✖ = Set appointment, booked a class, etc. . . . made a sale

This approach answers the following questions:

1. Am I picking up the telephone and dialing at all?

2. When dialing, am I making contacts?

3. When I am making contacts, do I have the skills to set appointments or close sales?

When making calls, note the times the calling session begins and ends. This is best tracked in an appointment box. Completing this is critical to determining the best time to reach people on the telephone. Look for a trend and discover which call times yield the most contacts (that is, those you marked with a slash or an X). Use this method for 30 days to pinpoint your **prime calling times**. Knowing your prime calling times and tracking your activity helps you pick up the phone with purpose. They lead to becoming a more focused telephone professional.

Advanced Tracking Methods

If a telephone and computer are utilized to generate most of your business, we suggest adding two additional tracking techniques. If voice mail is left or an e-mail message is sent, simply draw a vertical line through the dial. If information is sent to your contact, but no appointment set, put a square around the slash.

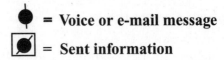

= Voice or e-mail message
= Sent information

Think of this square as an envelope just dropped in the mail. At the end of the day, look at the Call box to see your telephone activity at a glance. For example, the Call box below shows this individual made thirty-two calls, made eleven contacts, sent two information packets, and booked four appointments.

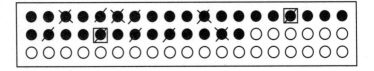

Knowing this information will help track and produce evidence of your activity. Over time, it will reveal if your efforts on the telephone actually work. The Call box provides instant feedback and gratification, especially when it shows a high level of activity. It provides accurate accountability—and it is fun and simple to use.

Which example illustrates your telephone activity last week?

Now that you know how the Call box works,
let's troubleshoot the following Call boxes below

Call reluctance and fear of the telephone
Solution: Start Making Dials

Making a lot of dials; not talking with many people
Solution: Change Your Call Time

Making a lot of dials; talking with many people, and not
getting requests for more info or closing sales
Solution: Use the 5-Step Phone Process

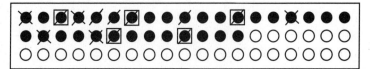

Making a small number of dials, talking with a lot of
people, getting requests for more info, and closing sales

It is not only important to produce evidence of activity, but to evaluate your effectiveness and skill level. For example, what assumptions would you make regarding the Call box displayed below?

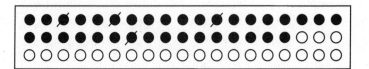

This call session would indicate that the caller lacked skills in two areas. First, the caller is not calling during prime calling times. Upon reviewing the evidence, no one is home at the time outgoing calls are being made. Only four people answered the telephone out of thirty-five calls. When telephone prospecting, it is important to call when the people are home so an actual appointment may be set. Advice: Try a different time daily until Prime Calling Times are determined. Secondly, the caller lacks effective communication skills. A telephone professional will book one appointment out of every second contact made or better. Step One explained clearly how to become a telephone professional: enhance your communication skills. See how easily problems are located and solutions applied? That is the power of the *Sales Success Planner*. Where performance is measured, performance is improved.

Let's try another example:

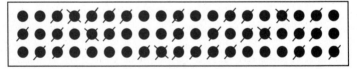

This caller has increased his or her telephone skills in one area. The caller targeted the best times to call: prime calling times. In this example, it was between six and eight p.m. on Thursdays. However, a problem still exists; the caller is only booking one appointment out of every five contacts. A telephone professional books one out of two. The solution? Go back to Step One and learn the telephone process.

Let's try another example:

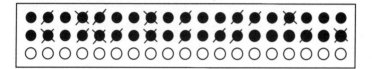

In this example, the caller not only called during prime calling times, but also mastered the telephone process, which in turn generated one appointment out of approximately every second contact (actually a call ratio of 1.8). The call ratio is excellent. This example illustrates a telephone professional. The tracking of activity made it easy to troubleshoot.

Whether you are monitoring your own sales performance or that of a team, using these concepts will produce evidence of activity and allow performance to be measured quickly and effectively. Knowing this information is vital to the success of any business. Experience in sales is not earned; it is learned. The quicker skills are mastered, the quicker financial goals will be obtained.

Your objective is to make the most contacts in the least amount of calls and get one appointment for every two contacts made . . . or better.

3. APPOINTMENT BOX

The six boxes below the Call box in the *Sales Success Planner* are for recording appointments, both business and personal, on a given day. Write in your contact's name, address, phone number, and other pertinent information.

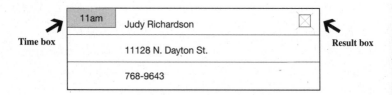

Unlike other planners, the *Sales Success Planner* has **Appointment boxes** that do not show preprinted times from dawn to dusk. Instead, in the shaded area at the top left, it provides a place to write in times for appointments. With only six boxes, this design gives enough space to write down only what is needed without feeling overwhelmed by too many empty boxes. Notice that it sets a standard for freedom and flexibility; like many home-based business owners, you probably rebel against daily planners controlling your life.

Be sure to include personal as well as business appointments in the Appointment boxes. Looking back on the day's and week's activity, you can quickly see the percentage of time devoted to Income Producing Activities. The Appointment box offers an additional tool not found in any other planner, the Result box. This box tracks and monitors appointment activity with the stroke of a pen. Mark your results in the Result box at the top right-hand corner of the Appointment box using the following codes:

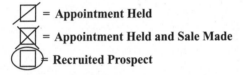

= Appointment Held

= Appointment Held and Sale Made

= Recruited Prospect

Rather than troubleshoot the Appointment box, we would like to share a real life example:

Mary Jones is a home-based business owner with a large, reputable NWM company. She began using the *Sales Success Planner* in an attempt to grow her business. She began tracking her activity and within two weeks she was startled to learn her closing skills were not as effective as once thought. Upon reviewing the evidence of activity, Mary could see that in two weeks' time she went on twenty-four appointments, but only closed ten of them with someone becoming a recruit. She could quickly review her activity by the coding in the Result box located in her planner. The tracking revealed Mary was working hard, but not smart. To increase her closing ratios, Mary created a Customer Profile sheet for both her products and recruiting and began to ask these questions to determine customer needs.

She quickly learned that good questions result in high commissions. Mary increased her closing ratio by 30 percent and her sales increased on average by 60 percent. She also spent less time on each appointment due to her increased focus and control. She now uses her completed Customer Profile sheets to contact customers on a regular basis in attempts to fill unmet or new needs. She also went back to all her previous customers and asked them questions to determine if any needs were previously neglected. This also created additional sales and increased her confidence in dealing with her customers. Mary now understands the importance of working smart, not hard, and the Result box of her *Sales Success Planner* keeps her aware of her skill level at all times.

Mary recently reviewed her tracking with us and she was proud to reveal that in the last two weeks she went on eighteen appointments and closed thirteen of them, with four becoing recruits. The Result box made it simple for her to produce this evidence and provided her with the recognition she so deserved.

4. WEEK END SUMMARY

On each Daily Task sheet, there is a Week End summary. This is where you tally the number of activity points (which you will learn about in the next step), total sales, and your call ratio. In the very back of the planner there is a tool called the Weekly Tracker. This sheet keeps track of your weekly activity throughout the course of a full year. At the end of each week, be sure to fill this out. Simply add up the number of calls, contacts, and appointments recorded during the week. Count the number of circles, slashes, and Xs to determine total calls, and then count the number of slashes and Xs to determine total contacts. Finally, count the number of Xs to determine appointments set. The Weekly Tracker will allow you to look for trends in your business and to see at a glance if you have maintained consistent activity over time.

Next, determine your Call Ratio by using the formula learned at the end of Step One:

# of contacts ÷ # of appointments = Call Ratio

For example, if you had twenty-four contacts and set six appointments in one week, your Call Ratio would be 24 ÷ 6 = 4:1. That means an average of one appointment is set for every four contacts made.

24 contacts ÷ 6 appointments = 4:1 Call Ratio

When call ratios are improved, you will work less and make more.

Each section within the *Sales Success Planner* has its own distinct purpose. When used in its entirety with the Activity Point System (next step), the planner leads to working less and making more. As you go on to the following chapter, you will see how activity points keep the focus on the activities that promote production, rather than focusing on the production itself (to order a *Sales Success Planner* from Dynamic Performance call 1.800.640.0688 or visit our website at www.TraciBild.com).

Tracking Activity

The Activity Point System (APS) empowers sales professionals to do more of what matters by linking activity with production. Developing an awareness and understanding of what creates production is probably the biggest benefit of the APS. It keeps you committed to performing Income Producing Activities: calling and seeing prospects. In this step, you will learn a system to connect your activity to meaningful production.

Often sales professionals only link accomplishment with production. Yet, in sales, you have no control over production, but you do have control over activity. Since activity generates sales, it is imperative to have a system that measures how activity connects with production. The APS does just that—it links activity to production, measured in a dollar amount. When using the APS, you will reap many rewards—and have fun, too. The APS helps to:

- Create a sense of accomplishment

- Develop successful work habits

- Keep you committed to activities that promote production

- Develop a better understanding of what creates production

- Answer the question: *"What amount of activity is required to achieve my goals?"*

I once received a letter from a woman named Justine, a sales professional who was just ten months into her career. She was desperately working to earn a top-performer prize: a free car! Justine had already once been on target to earn her free car and had fallen off prior to our meeting, so she was very discouraged. Justine had exhausted every avenue, attempted to sell to every friend, family member, and had pulled in all the favors she could think of to get new appointments. She even had leads from several lead-generating sources, but was not having success in converting those into appointments. The company Justine worked for provided great scripts, so she was never at a loss for words, but the scripts just were not working for her. Even the seventeen years she had spent in the mortgage industry, where she was very successful, had not prepared her properly to prospect or close sales. Justine was burning out.

After going through my training program, Justine realized she had a bad case of call reluctance. She had all the symptoms. She allowed herself to get distracted very easily and found numerous excuses to put off making prospecting calls. Now aware of her problem, Justine implemented the process learned in Step One and improved her call ratio to 1.8 (better than one out of two). She loved not having to use scripts; just good communication skills that she could put into practice right away. She no longer had to shy away from conversations because she no longer had to worry about overcoming objections, something she once hated. All she had to do was reveal her prospect's needs and share with him or her how she could fill them. It was so simple!

This was just the beginning. There was something else that really got Justine's attention. After learning the Activity Point System, she realized that it was the effort that mattered not the result. Her focus became the points, 1500 per week (you will learn about points in this step), and she knew she would earn her free dream car. It no longer mattered what prospects said because she got points just for talking to them. She knew that if she just got the points, the results would come. She also learned that by knowing and improving her call ratio, she could be confident that the bookings were right around the corner. Justine began to look forward to prospecting. "Could I beat my best day in points?" became her daily challenge.

The system presented in this book became Justine's

anchor to move her sales career forward. Just four months after attending my seminar to learn the techniques presented in this book, she earned her first free car. Four months after that she reached her initial goal, which was a promotion to sales director with her company. It has been three years since I first met Justine, and she is still driving her free car! This is testimony to the power of a system.

How The APS Works

Let's review how activity should be tracked when telephone prospecting and when holding appointments. The APS assigns points to specific business-building activities. The first way to earn points is by calling people: telephone prospecting. Each time you make a call, one point is earned. If contact is made with the prospect, you earn fifteen points. If an appointment is booked or a telephone sale is made, you earn fifty. If you send information regularly, you earn twenty-five points for each mailing done. Points are not added together, the highest points prevail. For example, if you make a call and speak with your prospect, it is fifteen points (not sixteen) because you made contact. The greater point level prevails. Below is how to track points.

Call box: APS At-A-Glance

Track your telephone activity by applying the following activity points:

⬤ = 1 point

◖ = 15 points

✖ = 50 points

▣ = 25 points

Notice how activity points are assigned to each tracking method: one point for a call, fifteen points for a contact, fifty points for setting an appointment, class or workshop, or making a sale over the phone, twenty-five points when information is sent to a contact. Tracking telephone activity and assigning points allows you to link activity with production. A higher level of activity leads to a higher level of production. You will find that, over time, earning activity points becomes habit-forming; it makes calling people fun.

The second way to earn points is by seeing people. That activity is recorded in the following way:

▱ = 15 points

⊠ = 50 points

⊡ = 100 points

Appointment box: APS At-A-Glance

Again, if you decide to use the *Sales Success Planner*,

the Appointment box below shows how you would
track your results in the Result box:

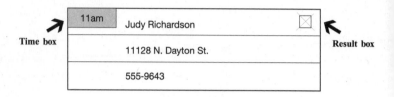

Again, see how points are assigned to each tracking
method? The Activity Point System makes a practical
connection between activity and production. In turn,
the tracking process provides a sense of accomplishment.
Where there is activity there is production. The Activity Point System makes tracking activities easy and fun.
Remember to shoot for activity to generate production.
For example, if you are in sales full-time or run a full-
time business, shoot for at least **1000 activity points**
a week. If your business is *on the side,* pursue **500 activity points** a week. These are general suggestions for
getting started and have been proven to get results in
multiple industries, from insurance to direct sales.

Do you see how this works? Collect activity points
and success will follow because you know you are doing
the activities that build your business: calling and
seeing prospects. Chasing activity points every day will
have an immediate impact on your business. It helps
you prioritize and distinguish between Income Producing Activities and nonincome producing activities.

When deciding which task to do first, ask yourself, *"Does this task earn me activity points?"* The more activity points earned, the higher production obtained. If your goal is to make money, make activity points a daily priority. In time, you will have a clear understanding of the correlation between activity and production. That makes it easy to put calling and seeing people your number one priority.

Formula for Success

In this chapter, we introduce the Formula for Success. A formula is nothing more than a recipe. This formula you are about to learn is for success and will help you answer the following question:

What amount of work is required to achieve my financial goals?

Many people prefer to estimate the level of work or activity necessary to achieve their financial goals. Some simply preach that long hours and much hard work is the answer. But just like any good recipe, the ingredients must be exact, or the end product will be different than expected. This is why we created the Formula for Success, so you will have the recipe and ingredients necessary to make your business or sales career a success.

Our formula proves once and for all that the number

one key to sales success is contacts. It also proves that years of experience are not necessary in order to achieve your financial goals. I believe most people that fall short of their goals simply were unaware of what amount of work was required to achieve that target. Consider the following:

Q. *What possesses people to put forth time and energy (be active) toward the accomplishment of someone else's goal?*

A. Wages.

We live in a society that is accustomed to wages, or payment for work, being paid in the form of pay-per-hour or a set salary (which still can be broken down to an hourly salary). Pay-per-hour makes it easy to achieve financial goals because it makes it easy to know what amount of work is required to achieve that goal.

Q. *How?*

A. By using equations.

The most commonly used equation to determine what is required to arrive at our financial goal would be:

GOAL ÷ WAGE = AMOUNT OF WORK

Consider someone who earns $20.00 an hour and wants to make $50,000 per year. To determine how many hours need to be worked this individual would divide their goal by their wage.

$50,000 annually ÷ $20.00 per hour = 2,500 hours in a year

To earn $50,000 this individual needs to have 2,500 hours within a year to arrive at his or her financial goal. This would be an average of about forty-eight hours per week. A person who knows and understands exactly what is required to arrive at a goal has a far greater chance of getting there than someone who lacks this valuable information. If you are a salaried worker, then determine what your average pay per hour is and use this figure to complete the equations taught in this step. For example, if you earn $4,000 per month in salary and work on average forty-eight hours per week (minus two weeks' vacation), your average pay per hour is $20.00.

Salaried example:
$48,000/year ÷ 2,400 hours/year (48 × 50 weeks) = $20/hour

What about you? If you knew exactly what amount of work was required to arrive at your goal, would you have a far greater chance of getting there?

Before revealing our formula and its secret ingredients, it is first important to clarify several misconceptions about sales. Remember:

- In sales, you are not paid for your time, you are instead paid for your activity.

- The only two activities that promote production and business growth are Income Producing Activities: calling and seeing prospects.

Because we get paid for our activity, we no longer have a *wage* and we can no longer use the equation because:

GOAL ÷ ? = ?

As a result of not knowing what amount of work is required to achieve their goals, many people get stuck in what we call the **P.O.P. Syndrome:**

P—Planning
O—Organizing
P—Prioritizing

- Because of not knowing what is required to achieve a goal, do you find yourself spending too much time **P**lanning, **O**rganizing, and **P**rioritizing?

- Due to the confusion over what kind of activities

really pay you and grow your business, do you
again find yourself **P**lanning, **O**rganizing, and
Prioritizing?

■ Is the time spent **P**lanning, **O**rganizing, and **P**rioritizing robbing you of the time needed to achieve
your financial goals?

Are you stuck in this P.O.P. Syndrome? In order to
learn and understand what activities really pay you and
grow your business, you must learn how to calculate
your wages. This step will help you do just that.
Tracking activity is critical if you want to utilize the
Formula for Success. You may use the method for
tracking that you already have in place, or you may use
our *Sales Success Planner*. The planner, when used in
its most basic form, will produce evidence of Income
Producing Activities performed. At its next level, it
helps you to associate activity with production. In its
highest form, the *Sales Success Planner* will provide the
ingredients necessary to calculate your wages, our *Formula for Success*.
Simply do the following:

■ Add up total sales, commissions or recruits for the
past 30 days.

■ Add up total activity points for the past 30 days.

■ Divide total sales, commissions, or recruits by total activity points to learn your wage.

SALES ÷ ACTIVITY POINTS = WAGES

or

$ ÷ AP = W

When used, this formula will reveal your wage so you can figure out what amount of work is required to achieve your financial goal. Once this is revealed, it is up to you to perform the activity necessary to make the goal a reality. Keep in mind, because you are in sales, your wage is not paid in salary or pay-per-hour. It is instead paid in the form of **pay-per-activity point**. As mentioned in Step Five, activity points are collected only when calling and seeing prospects. What happens when you enter sales or start a business? Most people, when making this career change, fail to realize a critical element is missing: wages. When trying to complete their familiar formula, it becomes impossible.

GOAL ÷ WAGE = AMOUNT OF WORK

GOAL ÷ ? = ?

How can this formula be completed without knowing your wage? It can't! This is why so many people in sales fail to realize their dreams. Instead of having a solid answer, they begin to enter the P.O.P. Syndrome. As mentioned previously, **P**lanning, **O**rganizing and **P**rioritizing cannot provide income because they are not Income Producing Activities. The only way to guarantee that income goals are accomplished is to put wages back into the formula. To learn what your wages are, you must utilize the following Formula for Success:

SALES ÷ ACTIVITY POINTS = WAGE

For example:

$1,000 ÷ 1000 activity points = $1.00/activity point

When calculated in the example above, this formula reveals a wage of $1.00 per activity point earned. Sounds strange doesn't it? Here is where the power in this formula comes in. Now that wages are determined, you can answer the question: *what amount of work is required to achieve a financial goal?*

GOAL ÷ WAGE = AMOUNT OF WORK

$50,000 ÷ $1 PER ACTIVITY POINT = 50,000 ACTIVITY POINTS / YEAR

To achieve $50,000 in annual sales, this person would need to earn 962 activity points per week (52 workweeks in a year not including vacations). And remember, the only way to earn points is by calling and seeing people. This formula provides a tangible plan for accountability and accomplishment of all financial goals. It will also reveal if goals are too high and unrealistic. Let's review some more examples:

USING WAGES IN THE FIELD

Jack tracks his activity for one month and learns the following:

Total sales = $2,000

Total APs = 2800 (700/week)
$2,000 ÷ 2800 = $.71/point
Wages = $.71/point

Jack sold $2,000 in product and earned a total of 2,800 activity points (APs) for the month. His goal is to sell $3,500 next month. With a Wage of $.71 per activity point, Jack determines how many activity points he needs to produce $3,500, his goal, in this way:

Goal ÷ Wage = activity points needed

or

$3,500 ÷ $.71 = 4,930/month (1,233 points/week)

Jack sees that he needs to almost double his activity from 2,800 to 4,930 activity points to meet his goal of $3,500 in sales.

———————

Sue tracked her activity and got these results:

Total sales = $3,000
Total APs = 3,200 (800/week)
$3,000 ÷ 3,200 = $.94/point
Wages = $.94/point

Her goal for the next month is $5,000. What amount of work must she do to meet this goal?

Goal ÷ Wages = activity points needed
$5,000 ÷ $.94 = 5,320/month (1,330/week)

To meet this goal, Sue must increase her activity next month by 2,120 points, from 3,200 to 5,320.

———————

Michelle tracks her activity for one month and learns the following:

Total sales = $5,000
Total APs = 6,000 (1,500/week)
$5,000 ÷ 6,000 = $.83/point
Wages = $.83/point

If Michelle sets a goal of $8,000 in sales, she needs to earn 9,639 activity points, or more than 2,500 a week. This may be unrealistic for her. Instead of increasing her level of activity, she could focus on increasing her wage per point instead. To do this, Michelle would make improving her telephoning and presentation skills her primary focus for the next few weeks.

———

David has used the Activity Point System for a full year. These are his results:

Total sales = $62,000
Total APs = 41,600 (800/week for 52 weeks)
$62,000 ÷ 41,600 = $1.49/point
Wage = $1.49/point

Next year, he intends to do $100,000 in sales. He uses the Formula for Success based on this year's production. At $1.49 per activity point, David has two choices to make his goal a reality. He can increase his activity to 1,291 points a week . . .

$100,000 ÷ $1.49/AP = 67,114 APs (1,291/week)

. . . or work on improving his wages per point by mastering the steps in this book.

WORKING LESS; MAKING MORE

What would happen to David (in the example above) if he chose to increase his wage instead of his level of activity? Remember, his goal is to work less and make more, which happens when you implement the first five steps. If David wants to maintain sales of $62,000 next year so he can spend more time with his family instead of growing to $100,000, he would do the following:

- Work diligently to become a telephone professional, obtaining one appointment for every two contacts . . . or better.

- Master face-to-face selling by finding needs.

- These two activities *alone* will increase David's wage. By doubling his current wage from $1.49/point to $2.98/point, David would then only need to earn 400 activity points a week—that's half the activity he performed the previous year. This means he would work only half as much to reap the same rewards! When he achieved this, he would be able to enjoy the true reward of financial success: TIME.

Now that we have reviewed these examples, let's do one more example of a person who is paid for their time. Pay-per-hour, or wages, makes it easy to know what amount of work is required to achieve financial goals.

GOAL ÷ WAGES = AMOUNT OF WORK

Consider an individual who earns $20 per hour and wants to make an income of $50,000 annually. To determine the amount of work required to achieve this goal, divide the income goal by wage per hour:

$50,000 ÷ $20 = 2,500 hours per year

To earn the desired $50,000 per year income, this individual must work 2,500 hours over the course of the year. This averages about forty-eight hours per week. Is this realistic? Of course it is. A person who knows and understands exactly what is required to arrive at a financial goal has a far greater chance of accomplishing it than someone who lacks this valuable information.

Dynamic Performance has revolutionized the sales industry by helping individuals put wages back into the equation. The key difference is that instead of wages being in the form of pay per hour, they are in the form of pay-per-activity point. Wages let you know how many activity points are required to meet goals. Remember, the only way to earn Activity Points is by calling people and seeing people. Use goals to determine activity, but focus on the activity itself to be successful. After tracking activity and sales for a minimum of thirty days, utilize the Formula for Success to determine your wage and to answer the question concerning what amount of work is required to accomplish the success that *you* desire.

Corporate businesses and top producers know and understand wages; they've used them for decades. Using wage-per-activity point might be the best-kept secret in America for sales professionals and home-based businesses.

Why has this secret stayed hidden? Because there has never been a fun, easy-to-use, quick way of tracking individual activity—until now. The *Sales Success Planner* and Activity Point System make learning and using the *Formula for Success* easy. Your goal is to determine a wage (the dollar value for every activity point) to understand what amount of work is required to achieve your goals and dreams.

Just six weeks into using the steps taught in this book, Tammy, a consultant in a Fortune 500 direct selling company sold $3,000 in product, sponsored five new team members, and earned $1,460 extra for recruiting with commissions, bonus, etc. Tammy made 158 contacts during this time, which, after using the *Formula for Success*, taught her that she was earning approximately $17.00 for each contact she made. Additionally,

Tammy found that she is now able to stay focused daily on the activities necessary to grow her business. And being the recognition-oriented person that she is, she got personal satisfaction at the end of the day for a good day's work; visually she could see what had been accomplished. Lastly, being the workaholic that she is, Tammy now has a measuring tool to go by to say to herself, "It's okay, you can take a break now." Whereas before she would work and work and work and often become nonproductive. This system made a permanent impact on Tammy's business and she recommends that everyone put it to use, it's just that powerful. She feels that if everyone in sales could be exposed to this training, it would change the complexion of the industry entirely.

Prospecting

Now that you know what to say when calling on prospects and you know how to reveal their needs, whom exactly do you call? In sales, it is critical to have a constant flow of prospects to whom you can market your services. There are many ways to generate leads—some are effective and some are not. To help you reach your desired level of income, maintain it and even exceed it, you must learn the most productive way to obtain prequalified prospects on a regular basis. Here are several popular ways to generate leads. Keep in mind I said popular, not best:

- Make a list of 100 people you know

- Hand out business cards wherever you go

- Buy a leads list

- Join a networking group

- Go to trade shows

These methods will produce a good number of leads for you. But the best way to obtain leads is through referrals. Who better to sell your services than a satisfied client sending a friend your way? This referral is what I call red hot. Not only did he or she recommend your services to a friend, there is already a feeling of trust between two friends. Rather than trying to gain trust, which could take months if not years, the person who referred you has already established that trust for you.

Word of mouth is the best advertising you can possibly have. So how do you get your trusted clients, friends, and business associates to provide you with referrals? The answer is simply to ask! At the end of your appointment, whether the person is a current client or prospect, whether they buy or not, pull out a blank piece of paper. Write the numbers five through one in descending order on the paper, and turn it around so the client you are sitting with can see it.

Let's pretend that I am an insurance agent and I just met with Jack, a father of four, who has expressed an interest in a whole life insurance policy. Jack has not purchased my products or services yet; he has only met with me. I now need to go back to my office and prepare a policy that will fit his needs. In any event, we schedule another appointment for the following week to review my proposal. However, before I leave the initial appointment, I will ask for referrals. Again, do not wait to see if this person is going to buy from you. Referrals are money in the bank. Here is a sample of what I might say, *"Jack, the best way I can grow my business is through referrals. Could you just jot down five people you know that have children, that I can call and introduce myself to for future reference?"*

Why did I say *"people that have children?"* It is important that I make this task mentally and psychologically simple for Jack. If I were to ask him whom he knew that needed or could benefit from life insurance, what do you think he would say? His response would be: *"I need to think about it,"* or *"I can't think of anyone at this time,"* or *"I'm sure all my friends already have their own insurance agent."* Have you heard these things before when asking for referrals?

The key is keeping it simple. Maybe Jack really does not know anyone who might need life insurance, but if instead you asked Jack who he knows that has children, he will probably ramble off about five or six names. When using this approach, you are not asking Jack to endorse you or your services. You are instead asking him the simple question of who he knows that has children? What this does for you is instantly prequalifies referral prospects—lots of them. These are people who have children, more than likely a spouse, and a friend is referring them to you. Birds of a feather flock together. If Jack has insurance needs, his friends with children probably do, too.

When asking this referral question, take out a piece of paper and turn it around for the prospect with the numbers five through one in descending order. Then say, *"Would you mind writing down the names and numbers of five people you know who have children that I can call and introduce myself to for future reference?"* This implies that you are not going to go run to their friends and try to sell them insurance. It also implies that you are just interested in a handshake or introduction should they need your services in the future. Mentally, Jack can handle this. Psychologically, he sees the numbers in descending order and if he has filled in the first two names, he is going to work diligently to list the remaining names. Here is how your list will look:

5. _____

4. _____

3. _____

2. _____

1. _____

It is important that your list be in descending order. By nature people like to complete tasks and leaving this list incomplete would bother many people, which is good for your lead bank! If the list reads one through five in ascending order, psychologically, there will not be such a need to complete the list, there is no challenge other than to list up to five but not necessarily all five. Your objective when asking for referrals is to get your clients to think about common interests that they might have with friends or business associates. Here are several different types of examples:

- Stockbroker: *"Whom do you know that invests in the stock market or that has talked about investing in the stock market at some point in their life, that I can call?"*

- Recruiter: *"Whom do you know that needs extra income that I can call?"*

- Car Salesman: *"Whom do you know that trades their car in every couple of years that I can call?"*

- Real Estate Agent: *"Whom do you know that owns a house and has talked about upgrading in the next several years that I can call?"*

Now, here is the power in this system. If you want to sell more than ever before, ask the person who just gave you these names to tell the people on the list that you may be calling and that you only want to introduce yourself to them for future reference. This is very non-threatening and may even make your client feel better about having given you their names. I call this *activa-*

tion, which means to make active or cause to engage in activity. Once a prospect is activated, you can count on an appointment being set.

Imagine the following:

- You're at home cooking dinner and someone cold calls in hopes of selling you an insurance policy. How do you react? Typically you are offended that this person called and work to get them off the telephone as quickly as possible.

- Now imagine that instead of a cold call, this same insurance agent called you and said that your friend Sally suggested he give you a call. You would probably feel a little better and more trustful of the person calling. However, you may still find a good reason not to schedule an appointment.

- Now, picture yourself again cooking dinner and Sally calls you herself to tell you that she just met with an insurance agent, Jack in this case, who was extremely professional and very helpful. She also tells you that she gave him your name so he could introduce himself should you ever need his services in the future, and he will most likely be calling.

The next day, Jack calls to introduce himself and schedule an appointment. How do you think you would then respond? You, like most people would agree to the appointment. Jack comes highly recommended. He was professional on the telephone and it seems harmless to meet with him. If you could run your business on the premise of obtaining prequalified referrals that were *activated* by the person giving them, how much do you think your business would grow? This method of prospecting will keep you so busy that you will never have to prospect in any other way. This means you will not have to join clubs that you would never typically join but do so just to obtain leads. No more expenses spent on purchasing lead lists and no more fret over who you are going to call. Referral leads are the best, and they are free!

Be sure to send the person who provided you with referrals a thank-you card. Each time you obtain a new client because of the referral, provide another thank-you card or small gift of appreciation. This will make your client or prospect happy that he or she initially provided you with referrals and make it much easier to provide you with more as they come to mind. Now, remember, this person may or may not be a client of yours. Imagine if this person has not done business with you yet, suddenly, his or her friends and business associates are. You will earn a client in due time, this person will become very loyal to you, and your name will be the catalyst of many future conversations where, again, more referrals will appear.

Let's review what we would say when calling on a referral. Always use the five-step telephone system. This is an example of a real estate agent calling on a referral prospect.

"Hi, is Janet in?"

"This is she."

"Hi Janet, this is Lili Jones calling."

"Yes."

"I understand that you're a good friend of John White."

"Oh, yes I am!"

"Do you have a quick minute?"

"Sure."

"Janet, the reason I'm calling is because I am a real estate agent with Sun Coast Realty and John said some great things about you. He also said that you were currently thinking about selling your home and purchasing something a little bigger. I would be very interested in meeting with you to share the benefits of my services and wondered what might work best in your schedule to get together, weekdays or weekends?"

"Well, John did tell me that you would be calling and told me what a great job you did in helping his family locate their new home. I would love to meet with you. Are you free tomorrow night around six?"

"That would work great, may I get your current address?"

This call would end with you obtaining her address and confirming the appointment time. Make it a point to never ask for directions. Purchase a city map and keep it in your car. A telephone conversation can go very well and then, when asking for directions, everything that you just worked so hard for is damaged. As you may know yourself, directions tend to get difficult to explain or may be an inconvenience for the prospect to provide. If you have an idea of where you are going and just want to confirm the directions, then it's fine to ask.

Now, let's review an example of an *activated* prospect that objects to meeting with you.

"Hi, is Jeff in?"

"This is he."

"Hi Jeff, this is Hope Smith calling."

"Oh, hello. Troy said you would be calling."

"I understand you're about to retire!"

"Yes, I am."

"Do you have a quick minute?"

"Yes, real quick, I'm about to go for a run."

"Jeff, the reason I'm calling, as Troy may have mentioned, is because I am a consultant with Johnson & Company. Troy had said some great things about you and also said

that you are about to retire and that you have a great knowledge of computer programming. I am currently searching for a qualified candidate to do part-time consulting work with one of my best clients. I wondered if you might have a minute that I could ask you a few brief questions?"

"I appreciate Troy's confidence in me, but I really am not interested at this time. Thanks for calling and for thinking of me."

"I do understand, Jeff. While I have you on the telephone, may I ask you one quick question?"

"Sure."

"Once you retire, what do you plan to do with your free time after working all these years?"

"Well, I'm not sure. I do know that I'm not going to just sit around and get lazy like many of my friends have done once they retired. I plan to find some part-time, easy work, and just enjoy my freedom."

"May I ask what is most important to you in regards to the part-time job you decide to take?"

"Well, I want a job that is not demanding of all my time and one that pays me a decent income. I definitely want the flexibility in hours that I have never had."

"Well, Jeff, that is actually one of the reasons I was hoping to visit with you. A number of consultants I have con-

tracted with have had the same concerns as you, especially where freedom and flexibility is concerned. They too felt a good income upon retiring was important to their overall decision. I would like to get together and share how I helped them. What might work best for us to get together, early mornings or afternoons?"

"Well, if we're going to do this, let's make it early. How about Tuesday around 8:00 a.m.?"

"That would be terrific, Jeff. Let me tell you where my office is . . ."

Imagine if this last referral had not been *activated*. Hope Smith may not have been able to schedule an appointment at all. The credibility Hope received from Troy made this appointment possible along with the identification of Jeff's needs. I think you can see how much more powerful it is when the person who referred you actually calls ahead. However, if they do not call, you will still have tremendous success, so do not wait too long to make contact.

When working with referrals and combining the five-step telephone system, you will always book one appointment out of every second contact or better. Referral prospecting will immediately impact your sales and allow you to work smart, not hard. Not only does this allow you to earn ten times the profit at less than one fifth the cost of other prospecting methods, it allows you to capture 25 percent of your potential lost by not referral prospecting.

I encourage you to start referral prospecting today, do not wait and do not let fear rob you of your dreams. At each appointment held, ask for referrals and go back through your current customer base and ask them, too. Once you implement this system into your business, you will never lack for prospects again and no other method for obtaining prospects will compare.

A Referral Worth $100,000

I used this referral prospecting method to grow my speaking business to levels I never dreamed possible. When I first started my business, I would speak for free to anyone who was willing to listen. About six months into my business I began to ask for referrals, and when I asked, I requested that the referrer take a moment and call my potential client and put in a good word for me—what I now call *activation*. Less than six months into using this referral method, I went from doing three to four free seminars in Florida per month to over 100 per year nationally at a generous full fee. Without this method there is no way I could have made the connections I did. The most recent example I can give you is a seminar I did for a large group of women business owners. As always, I asked for referrals, what I call "Dare to Share" at my events. I dare people to share my program with others by referring my services to those they think would benefit, just as I have taught you to do in this step. A few weeks later, before I had the opportunity to follow up on my referrals, one of them called me. A new start-up wanted to meet with me regarding a consulting opportunity. The person who had given me the referral had called as I requested and *activated* my new referral prospect. They were so excited by her feedback that they put a call in to me. That referral now amounts to over $100,000 per year in business. The question I want you to think about is, what if I had never asked? What if the person referring me had never *activated* the prospect? Imagine what this process can do for your business!

Making Miracles Happen

You never know when a miracle is right around the corner

The toughest challenge faced both in life and in running your business is creating workable processes that allow you to function or react in a positive, effective manner with little hesitation. Applying a process lets you train both mind and body to act without rethinking every step. It frees the mind from thinking about what is already known! This freedom increases the ability to comprehend and understand situations quickly and effectively because more mental energy is available.

It is easy to get overwhelmed when considering everything you want to accomplish. Yet, where you are in life is a direct result of your thoughts. And the future will be determined by the thoughts you have right now. If they are consumed day and night by trying to "hold it together," you will find yourself, years from now (and the rest of your life!), just trying to hold it together. Instead, if a process is created and dedicated to new exciting goals and a commitment is made to that process, you will shift from thinking burdensome thoughts to just doing what needs to be done! This in turn will allow room for more creative, forward-looking thinking. When using the power of thought for hope and looking ahead, you will move closer to your dreams. If your dream is to achieve financial success, for example, ask yourself these questions:

- How often do I think and dream about financial success and the freedom it brings?

- How often do I think about how to achieve this success?

- Have I created a process by which to carry out my plan of action (or do you keep asking yourself how you will merely get by)?

> *Thinking is the hardest thing to do, which is probably the reason why so few do it.*
> —HENRY FORD

Remember, creating a process dedicated to helping successfully grow your business is the biggest challenge you face. But the solution is simple: Simply use the steps presented in this book and expect miracles. I don't just believe, I know that financial success is readily available to everyone. I truly care about each and every person striving to make his or her dreams a reality. I care with all my heart because financial success is important.

There is a big reward for achieving financial success. That reward is *time*. And the greatest reward of time is the opportunity to build solid *relationships* in life. Your marriage will blossom, your children will achieve more from increased interaction with you, and your friendships will expand in number and enjoyment. An abundance of money is nice, but what does it matter if there is no one with whom to share it? This all leads to greater *happiness* in your life and, most importantly,

FREEDOM:

- Freedom to build and nurture meaningful relationships

- Freedom to know you can do and achieve anything in life you wish to pursue

- Freedom to know you control your own destiny

The Tools of Financial Freedom

Consider what this book can do for you. If you have tried some of the steps and tools that you have read

about but have fallen short, do not fret. You may not
have developed a clear understanding of the amount of
work required to ensure success. You may not have yet
determined wages for the activities that bring success.
To experience success in growing your business, make
it a priority to track and monitor the activities that
promote production, learn the Formula for Success, use
the Activity Point System to your advantage, and rely
on the *Sales Success Planner* or a comparable system to
keep focused. These systems work, and they will bring
the financial freedom you seek.

Get Ready to be Lucky

In Ernest Hemingway's *The Old Man and the Sea*, the
fisherman goes eighty-four days without catching a fish.
Yet, throughout that time, he stays focused on the process of fishing. He fishes in the right spots and he keeps
his lines precisely at the right depth. In this way, he
knows the drought he experiences is no fault of his
own. "I would rather be exact," the old man says.
"Then, when the luck comes, you are ready." Just as a
fisherman has tools, so do you. The Formula for Success,
the Activity Point System, and the *Sales Success Planner*
are the tools of champions. Use them to make the miracle of financial freedom happen in your life.

Here is an overview of the key concepts in the previous chapters.

STEP ONE—CALLING 101

To sell your product or service, making contacts is the number one key to sales success. The more people called, the more prospects seen, the more products sold, guaranteed. A process for mastering the telephone helps you set appointments that lead to sales. These steps are:

1. The Opening
2. Disarming
3. The Reason
4. Checkmate Question
5. Checkmate Close

It is natural for people to feel guarded when they receive a sales call. The Opening and Disarming steps allow you to elicit three yes responses in the first minute of the phone call. This in turn disarms the prospect and enhances the odds of getting an appointment. It also shows your professionalism, especially when permission to talk is obtained.

The goal of the Reason step is to obtain an appointment or an objection. In this step, identify the company you represent and the purpose of your call, saving detailed information for the appointment (unless you do not physically have to go on appointments). If the prospect objects to setting an appointment, do not get discouraged. Move on to the Checkmate Question to determine the prospect's highest need. Here, you not only prequalify prospects, but show your ability to listen.

The Checkmate Close is designed to make the prospect take action regarding your product or service. In this step an appointment is set based on particular needs stated by the prospect. If your business does not require appointment setting then the presentation is done in this step or an appointment is made to do one at a later date. Remember to focus on what is in it for the prospect, not for you. The more needs revealed, the more success obtained.

This process will forever change your life. When used effectively, it will produce one appointment out of every second contact . . . or better. Do not settle for less!

STEP TWO—APPOINTMENTS 101

This is where actual face-to-face selling skills begin. Or, if only doing telephone appointments, this is where the selling begins. When Shopper's State of Mind is applied, excitement is generated and prospects become open and receptive to your product or service. It gets them involved immediately and eliminates any skepticism. When involved, prospects form an impression based on your professional and caring attitude. This process influences the mind-set of your prospects and opens the door to identifying needs.

STEP THREE—FINDING NEEDS

Many sales professionals take a show-and-tell approach to selling. This not only undermines the buyer's needs but limits future business. When identifying needs it helps your prospects make an educated decision because it pinpoints unfulfilled needs. Only when needs are understood can an appropriate recommendation be made. Only when these needs are filled will your prospects continue to reorder and refer your services to their friends. This is the greatest service you can provide both to your prospects and current customers.

STEP FOUR—PRODUCING ACTIVITY

The *Sales Success Planner* is the first planner designed specifically for the home-based business owner and sales professional. It will not only help organize your life, but keep you focused on the activities that promote production: calling and seeing prospects.

As goals are set, the *Sales Success Planner* tracks and monitors the activities necessary to achieve them. Visual accountability to the effort put forth to grow your business is the greatest aspect of our planner. And to accomplish any goal, knowing what amount of work is required to guarantee an on-time arrival is critical.

The key sections to the *Sales Success Planner* are:

■ Daily Task Sheet

- Call box

- Appointment box

- Week End Summary

- Activity Point Totals

When used in its entirety, these sections will pinpoint the strengths and weaknesses of your business and help maintain consistency. Weekly totals are tracked in the Weekly Tracker, located in the back of the *Sales Success Planner*, allowing you to see the growth of your sales or business at a glance.

STEP FIVE—TRACKING ACTIVITY

The Activity Point System (APS) holds sales professionals accountable to Income Producing Activities: calling and seeing people. Tracking activity points keeps the focus on performing the activities that promote production. This system creates consistent monthly activity levels so you will not have to scramble to meet month-end goals.

Points are earned for every contact made, whether on the telephone or in person. Set a point goal every week and keep on top of it daily. Activity points are earned by:

Calling People

Dial   1

Contact   15

Appointment 50

Seeing People

Presentation 15

Sale   50

Recruit   100

Strive for 500 activity points per week if you are part-time and 1,000 a week if full-time. Go for 1,500 points and watch miracles happen in your life! To learn exactly how many activity points are required to reach your desired financial goal, simply learn your wage.

STEP SIX—FORMULA FOR SUCCESS

Combined with the *Sales Success Planner* or a tracking method of your choice, the Activity Point System and the Formula for Success allows you to determine wages in order to determine the amount of work necessary to meet your goals. This simple formula links activity points to production, measured in a dollar amount.

$ ÷ AP = WAGES

Total sales ÷ Total activity points = Wages

Using this formula allows you to complete the equation you have used most of your life to achieve financial goals by putting wages back into the equation:

GOAL ÷ WAGES = AMOUNT OF WORK

This identifies exactly how many activity points must be earned on a weekly, monthly, or annual basis to achieve any financial goal you set. It is up to you to determine whether that goal is realistic. If it is not, go back through the book and implement the techniques learned and gradually work toward bigger goals.

Remember: Your main focus should be to set and achieve realistic goals.

STEP SEVEN—PROSPECTING

Take the time to generate leads from people you meet on a daily basis. Many people in sales find it difficult to prospect because they have no one to call. Referral prospecting is the most effective type of prospecting and should be taken very seriously. Be sure to activate your referrals. Again, this means that the person who referred you actually calls or e-mails your new prospect and lets them know that you may be calling. Take the time to ask each person you meet with for a minimum of five referrals of people they know who have common interests and have them list these five names in descending order.

Starting Schedule

Renewals, reorders, team commissions, and so on, are gravy in your business. What grows your business are the activities tracked in the Call box and Appointment box. Putting more effort toward these Income Producing Activities will yield more gravy!

Here's a suggested schedule to get you started on using the entire system.

First 30 days

- Track your activity (in some way).

- Add up activity points each day and calculate totals for the week.

- Stay on top of tasks in the Daily Task sheet or your daily To Do's.

- Complete the Week End summary each week.

Days 31–60

- Keep doing everything you did during the first 30 days.

- Start calculating call ratios (e.g., 28 contacts ÷ 7 appointments = 4:1 ratio).

- Focus on improving your call ratios.

- Determine Prime Calling Times in order to reach the most people in the shortest period of time.

Days 61–90

- Keep doing what you learned in the first 60 days.

- Focus on Shopper's State of Mind and Finding Needs.

- Add up total sales and total activity points.

- Divide total sales by total activity points to calculate wage per activity point.

- Set your goals for the next 90 days and use wage-per-activity point to determine the number of activity points needed to achieve your goal (sales goal divided by wage equals amount of activity points necessary annually to achieve your goal. Divide this annual goal by fifty-two to determine points needed per week).

END OF FIRST YEAR

In the back of the *Sales Success Planner* is a Weekly Tracker where weekly totals are to be recorded. At the end of one year, add up your total sales, and then divide by total activity points to determine wages per point for the year just completed. Use this wage to set activity point goals for the coming year. If you do not use the recommended planner, make a chart to track your activity weekly for the year.

Your goal is to use wages to set high yet realistic goals for the future.

THE TIME IS NOW

Congratulations! Now that you have learned the *7 Steps to Successful Selling* and have an action plan, it is time to realize your dreams. Remember that it takes time to create new habits, but the rewards gained will far outweigh the pain. Each aspect of this training is based on specific steps. If you get confused, simply go back and start at Step One, Calling 101.

You have the opportunity to accomplish anything your heart desires. So few people realize how precious life is. Seize the day, each and every one, and let nothing stand in your way. Do not wait to start this system, do it today. Once implemented in its entirety, this seven-step system will allow you to reach your desired level of income, maintain it, then exceed it, all while learning to work less and make more.

Would You like to have Traci Bild Train Your Sales Force?

Although the 7 *Steps to Success Selling* is geared to sellers, the system works for anybody who needs to communicate effectively to accomplish their goals—from sales professionals increasing their income, to customer service representatives creating better service, to charities increasing their contributions! Virtually anybody can get more out of business, and out of life, with the 7 *Steps to Successful Selling*. So confident is Dynamic Performance in their system that their training includes a money-back guarantee. If our training does not boost productive results at least 10 percent, however results are measured, Dynamic Performance will make a full refund of fees. We are constantly adding to Dynamic Performance's catalog of quality products, which now includes the *Sales Success Planner*, audio and videotapes, books, and booklets.

Call or write Dynamic Performance today to find out how America's most dynamic professional development company can help you reach the level of success you desire, step-by-step!

Dynamic Performance International, Inc.
P.O. Box 26471
Tampa, FL 33623
1-800-640-0688
(local) 727-669-6830
fax 727-669-3921
www.TraciBild.com
traci@tracibild.com